Pica Pau 3

Animal Friends of Pica Pau 3
Gather All 20 Quirky Amigurumi Characters

© **2022 Meteoor BV (BE0550756201)**

Third print run, June 2023

First published November 2022 by
Meteoor Books, Antwerp, Belgium
www.meteoorbooks.com
hello@meteoorbooks.com

Have you made characters with patterns from this book?
Share your creations on
www.amigurumi.com/4100 or on
Instagram with #animalfriendsofpicapau3

Photography: Yan Schenkel & Matías Gorostegui
Illustrations: Yan Schenkel

Printed and bound by Grafistar

ISBN 9789491643446
D/2022/13.531/4

A catalogue record for this book is available from the
Royal Library of Belgium.

YAN SCHENKEL

ANIMAL FRIENDS OF

METEOOR BOOKS

INDEX

Here we are again. My third/fourth (and first?) book of crocheted critters. Yes, it's complicated. It's my third book in English, it will be my fourth in Spanish and French, but this book has some reworked animals that were part of my first. It's like a new music album with remastered old tunes and a bunch of new songs!

Many years have passed, and my way of crocheting toys has evolved. Alike many crocheters, I used to sell my makes. Selling my handmade toys was my full-time job for about 9 years. For this reason, my original patterns were simpler and thus faster to crochet in large quantities. I must have crocheted hundreds and hundreds of toys (I made Lucas fox at least 500 times!). I knew the patterns by heart so I could crochet arms, ears, and heads to fill any empty moment (I was often caught crocheting on public transport).

So, I was a full-time mom and in my "spare-time" I worked as crocheter, designer, photographer, and social media manager. Oh! and I was having a book published. My first book, "El mundo de Pica Pau" ("The world of Pica Pau") was released in my home country Argentina, back in 2015.

And yes, I was proud of being able to juggle all those balls, it felt like my superpower. But, at the same time, I was tired all the time and I wasn't enjoying my craft anymore. The hobby that had become a side job which then became my full-time job, gradually started to consume my creative energy... So, I stopped and asked myself what I wanted in life.

I realized that what made me happiest was designing, drawing, experimenting until this vivid idea I had in mind came to life. I could enjoy days crocheting a new piece until I got it just right (all while watching my favorite TV-series and movies, obviously). I also loved teaching, not only techniques and stitches, but teach others to find that fragile balance between self-criticism and self-patience, to be kind to ourselves, especially during a learning process.

We are all absorbed with the idea of having to be productive all the time, having the result as soon as possible, even in our spare time. We do not allow ourselves to slow down and truly observe. We are not able to let our work rest a night so we can gain perspective. Or to stop and enjoy the view (and even smell the roses, if you can). It is essential to understand where you are standing and what it is that you want in your life. On a smaller scale, slowing down has benefits as well. A crochet project that does not turn out the way we want, or with a new technique or stitch that we do not fully grasp, can cause frustration. We need to slow down, learn to handle this frustration and our urge to do everything economically - fast and efficient. We cannot be productive 24/7, even in our spare time or hobbies.

Many years ago, when I was studying arts, a teacher used to tell me: "let the work rest". One day, one week, one month. Let it rest, take the time to look at your work with rested eyes, a fresh head. Only then you decide if it's worth continuing, if you should redo a part, or throw it away and start over again. You must allow - and enjoy - the learning process.

So, to keep it short (or not): SLOW DOWN. We are here to learn, to enjoy the journey. We crochet. It's a manual process that involves our entire body - the tension, the touch, the movement when making each stitch, our thoughts, the tension (again), our breathing. This pastime allows us to create, with only a thread of yarn and a hook, stitch by stitch. And that in itself is marvelous.

WHEN CROCHETING MY PATTERNS

As with my previous books, this one is also divided into two main areas: a tools, basic stitches and techniques section, followed by the patterns. It's important to keep in mind that the skill level listed with a pattern is often subjective. Maybe you feel more comfortable crocheting the four-legged Eduardo Cutesaurus, than making the jacquard for the face of Ron Red Panda. And I'm guessing that you will simply begin with the one character that stole your heart, regardless of the skill level.

In addition to the basics in the first part of the book, you will find tips, techniques and step by step pictures throughout the book. While working in one pattern, I may refer back to the techniques in a previous pattern.

Practice every new stitch, every new technique, until you move your hands without thinking. Take your time, find your own pace. If you are new to crochet, make hundreds of chain stitches until you try the next stitch. Allow yourself the time to enjoy the process of learning a new craft.

Remember that there are no hard rules about stitches or techniques. Do what you find most comfortable or most natural, do YOU. But, if you really want your toys to look like the ones in the photos, there a couple of things that I can share:

What kind of single crochet stitch are you making?
There are two versions of the basic stitch when making toys. Which one is the best? Neither. Or both. I want you to know both and recognize them, so you can choose intentionally and are aware that the result will be different.

When I make my toys, I crochet them with the X-shaped single crochet, the "yarn under" single crochet, which looks like an X or cross. This stitch is more compact because you twist the yarn when you make that first yarn under. Your result will be a tighter and smaller stitch, and thus a more compact toy. Toys made with X-shaped single crochet are likely going to be a little longer than wide, and the fabric will be less fluid.
There's also quite a difference when making color changes. The X-shape is much like a square, like a pixel, and sometimes these stitches seem to align better. When crocheting jacquard patterns, the line between the color changes will seem straighter. But beware, if there are many rounds of color changes, you will always see that line turning to one side at some point, because you are working in spirals. Please, try to embrace the "imperfection". Yes, I know it's difficult, but it's part of our craft.

Second, you have the V-shaped single crochet, the more classic "yarn over" stitch. This results in a more fluid fabric and a softer toy, probably bigger, a bit wider and less tall. Keep in mind that these characteristics go for all the pieces you crochet. A snout crocheted with the X-shape will look thinner and longer than one crocheted in V-shaped single crochet.

You can find more info on how to make the X or V-shaped single crochet on page 24.

What yarn do you use?
I use cotton yarn, a particularly thick one, which would fall into the worsted weight category (100 g/170m). Any other yarn weight you may use will, obviously, change the size of the finished toy. And, if you are using acrylic yarn or wool,

your toy will be less rigid, fluffier, because these yarns are more elastic. So, if you decide to use a V-shaped single crochet with acrylic or wool, the toy might be fluffier, rounder, and bigger than the ones you see in my book. And that's perfect too.

The tension

Oh! The tension! This one is difficult because it's the one variable that is close-to-impossible to change... at least at first. And that's why I always recommend changing hook sizes instead of trying to change your natural tension.

When I started crocheting toys, I squeezed my stitches because I was afraid the fiberfill would show through. I made my stitches so tight that my hands hurt from tensing them and trying to get the hook through this compact and dense fabric. And my hands, my whole body, didn't feel relaxed at all.

With time, I started to loosen up my stiches, I became more relaxed. Basically, I started to crochet more confidently, almost without thinking. Now, after many years of crocheting every single day, I can control the tension a little more and switch yarn weights without changing the hook size. But there is always one combo of yarn and hook that works best, and in my case, this is worsted weight yarn with a 2.75 mm crochet hook.

If I could give you only one piece of advice, it is for you to experiment.
- Try both ways of making the single crochet... maybe you even find a third.
- Try different yarns and yarn weights. In fact, if you have the time, make two version of the same piece using cotton yarn and acrylic or wool, same yarn weight, same

crochet hook, so you can feel which one you prefer.
- And continue playing, trying out hooks and yarns, so you may find that perfect match that allows your natural tension to flow without effort. With time and practice you will notice that your stitches are neater, that the fabric is more even, and your hands don't hurt anymore.

And always remember that you are making HANDMADE toys. There will never be two crocheted pieces that look exactly the same. Imperfection is inevitably part of the process.

Tension for clothes and accessories

With a little practice, your tension for amigurumi will become consistent. You merely need to use the right crochet hook to get a tight but fluid fabric.

However, if you want to make matching clothes for your stuffed toys, it can be important to test whether the outfit will fit while crocheting. Many crocheters have different tensions when they crochet in rounds or rows. You don't want to find out at the very end that you've crocheted a pair of pants a few sizes too big.

If you notice that the outfit is getting too big, you can pick a smaller crochet hook to make your crochet fabric a little tighter and therefore smaller. If, on the other hand, the clothes become too small, it would be advised to use a slightly larger crochet hook to make your crochet fabric a bit looser and therefore larger.

Some outfits in this book are crocheted with a thinner yarn. Make sure not to overlook this detail.

AMIGURUMI GALLERY

With each pattern, I have included a URL and a QR code that will take you to that character's dedicated online gallery. Share your finished amigurumi, find inspiration in the color and yarn choices of your fellow crocheters and enjoy the fun of crocheting. Simply follow the link or scan the QR code with your mobile phone. Phones with iOS will scan the QR code automatically in camera mode. For phones with Android you may need to install a QR Reader app first.

TOOLS AND SUPPLIES

Every experienced crocheter has her/his favorite tools and materials, in addition to a well-formed opinion on the best techniques and the things you should always avoid. Of course, as in any other aspect of life, we do not always agree. Although each one of us has their own taste and point of view, we all acknowledge that one of the most wonderful things about crochet is that with basic tools and a strand of yarn you can create almost anything. The only thing that you need to keep in mind is that high-quality hooks and yarn can save you hours of frustration. Whenever possible, choose quality over quantity. Hooks and needles do have the habit of getting lost, so make sure you always have a backup, especially of the ones you love and use all the time.

CROCHET HOOK

Note: I didn't try all the hooks available on the market and it's impossible for me to estimate exactly what kind of hook will be the best for you. This is a quest you must follow all by yourself. But I do not want to leave you entirely in the dark, so I'm going to tell you what I have learned these past 13 years crocheting toys.

You may have noticed that, apart from different sizes, crochet hooks come in different materials. The choice for a material depends on your own preference. However, if you are planning to use cotton yarn, I strongly recommend working with **stainless steel** or **aluminum** hooks. Aluminum hooks are a great choice as they slip easily between stitches, are super light and come in the widest range of sizes. The thinnest aluminum hooks (less than 4 mm) might bend if you apply a lot of pressure, which happens when crocheting tightly. To avoid this, choose the ones with silicon, plastic, wood or bamboo handles or go for a stainless-steel hook (my personal favorite, as I tend to be a little rough on them).

Wooden and **bamboo** hooks are gorgeous and some brands have the most incredibly smooth finish, but I only recommend them if you are going to work with thicker yarns or crochet garments with looser stitches. The same goes for **plastic** and **acrylic** hooks, they're sometimes used to work with thicker materials, such as T-shirt yarn. I haven't tried these, as they seem less sturdy.

Besides the material of the hook, it's always wise to check the anatomy of the hook. As for the **point**: I prefer a rounded and blunt tip, with no rough edges so it doesn't split the yarn and slides through the stitches easily.

Also pay attention to the **throat** of the crochet hook. This part does the actual hooking (catching) of the yarn and allows you to pull it through the stitches and loops. You need a hook with a throat large enough to grab the yarn that you're working with, but small enough to prevent the previous loop from sliding off. This is especially important when crocheting toys, as you are going to use a crochet hook two or three sizes smaller than recommended for your yarn.

Another thing to keep in mind is the **handle**. I can say almost without a doubt that this is the most personal decision of all. In my case, as I hold the crochet hook like a knife (see page 18), I prefer to use crochet hooks without big handles. But if you hold it like a pencil, you will probably prefer the ones with an ergonomic or a rubber handle.

Hooks are like pens: we can crochet with any hook until we find the one that changes our lives. Yes, it's a bit dramatic, but it's true. And if it doesn't change your life, it will definitely change the way you crochet, especially if you do it all day long.

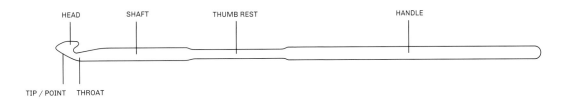

HEAD   SHAFT   THUMB REST   HANDLE

TIP / POINT   THROAT

Sizes

As a basic guide, a thicker thread needs a bigger hook and makes a larger stitch. If you crochet loosely, use a smaller hook to tighten your crochet fabric, and if you crochet tightly, use a larger hook to loosen your fabric. The hook size should be what's comfortable for you to use to obtain the desired result. It's easier to change the size of the hook than to modify the pressure you apply, as everyone tends to have a "natural" tension.

Hook sizes are indicated using different, land-specific systems, drawing on either numbers or letters or a combination of both. In the table below you can find the three most common systems in use: the metric system, the UK system and the US system. In this book I mention the metric and US size of the hook.

Crochet hook conversions

METRIC	UK	US
2 mm	14	-
2.25 mm	13	B-1
2.5 mm	12	-
2.75 mm	-	C-2
3 mm	11	-
3.25 mm	10	D-3
3.5 mm	9	E-4
3.75 mm	-	F-5
4 mm	8	G-6
4.5 mm	7	7
5 mm	6	H-8
5.5 mm	5	I-9
6 mm	4	J-10
6.5 mm	3	K-10.5
7 mm	2	-
8 mm	0	L-11
9 mm	00	M-13
10 mm	000	N-15

YARN

We can use almost any material that can be worked into a thread: wool, cotton, string, ribbon, fabric, leather, wire, even plastic bags or paper. Each kind of thread has its pros and cons. Allow yourself to experiment with different materials, it's the best way to learn and find what you like the most and what is most suitable for your project.

Always try to buy quality yarns, ones that are pleasant to the touch and comfortable to crochet with.

Cotton

Cotton is the most commonly used fiber for crocheting toys and, in my opinion, the one that gives the best result. It's a natural vegetable fiber made from cellulose. (Other threads composed of vegetable fibers are flax, jute, rayon, bamboo, hemp, etc.)

In addition to being a hypoallergenic material, cotton is extremely durable, easy to wash, very soft, and has plenty of color options to choose from! This thread has practically no elasticity, which is something you definitely want when making toys (so the toy keeps its shape). However, because of this lack of elasticity, the hook may not slide easily and sometimes, as cotton yarn is made up of several strands, the thread can be frayed by the hook.

You can find cotton threads in a variety of presentations: from more "rustic" and opaque ones, over shiny, mercerized cottons and combed ones (with threads that were combed to remove short fibers, to obtain more strength and softness).

Wools

Another type of natural fibers are the protein ones, the fibers that come from animal hair, like sheep's wool, alpaca, angora and mohair, or from insect secretions, like silk.

These yarns are more elastic than yarns made of vegetable fibers, so you have to keep in mind that toys made with this kind of yarn might lose their shape over time.

Beginners should avoid the hairiest ones (like angora and mohair), because the furry texture hides the structure of the fabric, making it harder to know where to insert the hook.

Synthetic fibers

Made of polymers, synthetic yarns are usually spun into a thread that resembles the texture and feel of animal fibers. Although they're cheaper and slip on the hook nicely, some tend to pill (form little fuzzballs on the surface) and create static. Nevertheless, it's one of the most commonly chosen yarns to make toys with because of the incredible range of colors. I myself am not such a big fan of the glossy finish, but, like everything in life, it's a matter of taste.

Fiber weight

The yarn's weight is its thickness, in other words the relationship between the weight and the number of meters. For example, a super fine thread used for lace may have about 800 meters in 100 grams, while a jumbo yarn, like the ones used for those super chunky blankets, may have less than 100 meters in the same weight. Internationally, most books and yarn manufacturers rely on standard terms to indicate yarn weight. The number of strands (or PLY) is mentioned optionally because an increase of plies doesn't mean that the yarn will be heavier (in fact, an 8-ply yarn formed of tightly twisted plies may be thinner than a loosely twisted 6-ply yarn).

NUMBER	NAME	TYPES OF YARN IN CATEGORY	PLY	m/100 gr	RECOMMENDED HOOK SIZE FOR GARMENTS (mm)
0	Lace	Fingering	1-2 ply	600-800 or more	1.5 - 2.5
1	Super Fine	Sock, Fingering, Baby	3-4 ply	350-600	2.25 - 3.5
2	Fine	Sport, Baby	5 ply	250-350	3.5 - 4.5
3	Light	DK (double knitting), Light Worsted	8 ply	200-250	4.5 - 5.5
4	Medium	Worsted, Afghan, Aran	10-12 ply	120-200	5.5 - 6.5
5	Bulky	Chunky, Craft, Rug	12-16 ply	100-130	6.5 - 9
6	Super Bulky	Super Bulky, Super Chunky, Roving		Less than 100	9 and larger
7	Jumbo	Jumbo, Roving		Less than 100	15 and larger

Note: The yarn weight and the hook should always relate to each other. Most importantly, always keep in mind that when making toys, you'll have to use a hook two or three sizes smaller than what is recommended for crocheting a garment (as stated in the table above). After all, we want a dense fabric that won't allow the stuffing to show through.

Note: The photo on page 17 shows the same character crocheted with 3 different yarn weights. The largest and original rabbit has been made with worsted weight yarn and a 2.75 mm hook. The middle one was made with DK weight yarn and a 2.75 mm hook. The smallest rabbit was made with fingering weight yarn and a 2.00 mm hook.

OTHER ESSENTIAL TOOLS AND SUPPLIES

Yarn and tapestry needles are used for joining motifs, sewing and finishing pieces. They have a blunt tip, so you don't split the thread or the crochet stitches. They also have a large eye that allows thicker yarns to pass through.

I have a thing for **scissors**, so I have a lot of them in different shapes and sizes. Choose a small, lightweight pair of scissors with sharp points.

A **stitch marker**, as the name suggests, is a tool used to mark a stitch. You can find them in a variety of shapes and qualities. Alternatively, you can use paper clips, safety pins or hair clips to help you indicate the round, row or any location on the worked piece.
When crocheting in rounds, always mark the first (or the last) stitch of the previous round.

I don't use a lot of **pins**, but they come in handy when you have to attach the head or limbs to the body of a toy. Try to get plastic or glass-headed ones: they're easy to spot in your crochetwork and their large head prevents them from slipping through the stitches.

For **stuffing** I always use polyester fiberfill, the same filling used to stuff cushions. It's easy to find in any craft shop, and it's inexpensive, washable and hypoallergenic. Stuffing a toy can be trickier than it seems: overstuffing might stretch the fabric and show through. Too little stuffing gives the toy a sad look, as if the poor thing was deflated. Try to insert small amounts at a time, adding more at a slow pace until you get the right look.

There is a great variety of extra elements to decorate crocheted toys: plastic eyes and noses in all colors and sizes, buttons, bows, ribbons, etc. For my characters, I only use **plastic safety eyes**. They have two parts: the front with a straight or threaded rod, plus a washer that goes inside the toy. If it's fastened correctly, it's practically impossible to remove. Be careful that the eye is where you want it to be before attaching it! If you're afraid that a tenacious child can pull them out, you can apply universal glue before placing them on the toy. Alternatively, you can embroider the facial features (especially if the toy is gifted to children under the age of three).

CROCHET INTRODUCTION

HOLD THE HOOK AND YARN (HAND POSITION)

Holding a new tool can be a little tricky, but a couple of hours of practice and a bit of patience will do the trick. If you already know how to crochet and you feel comfortable with it, stick to it! If you're learning, try as many ways as you like, so you can find the one most suitable for you. Usually, we handle the hook with the same hand we use to write, but it's not a rule. No matter how you hold the hook and the yarn, the most important thing you need to know is that there is no "best way" and definitely no "right way".

Pencil grip
Hold the hook as you would a pencil, grasping the hook between your thumb and index finger, in the middle of the flat section (the thumb rest).

Knife grip
Hold the hook in the same manner as you would hold a knife, grasping it between your thumb and index finger, resting the end of the hook against your palm.

Hold the yarn
The free hand is used to control the thread and hold the work. There are several methods to hold the yarn, and everyone has his or her preferred way. You only have to keep in mind that you have to maintain a steady tension while crocheting.

Holding the yarn is the real deal: you will need to practice controlling the thread and make the tension feel comfortable and natural. It's also important to keep this hand "in shape", because it's the one that's going to be stressed. Try to exercise before and after crocheting. I know it sounds almost impossible, but please, try not to crochet too many hours in a row!

  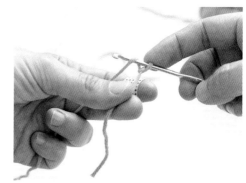

STITCHES

There are only a handful of basic stitches and although the variations and combinations are endless, you only need to master a few to make the patterns in this book. I will explain the stitches that I've learned throughout the years and still use. Always remember that you can and should adapt the techniques to your own needs and possibilities.

SLIP KNOT

The slip knot is the first loop you'll need to make on your hook to start crocheting. The slip knot does not count as a stitch.

1 Make a loop with the yarn tail. Insert the hook into it and draw another loop through.
2 Pull the yarn tail to tighten the loop around the hook.

CHAIN STITCH *(abbreviation: ch)*

This stitch is the basis for most crochetwork: if you are working in rows, your first row will be chain stitches, known as a foundation chain. The chain stitch is also used to join motifs and as a turning stitch.

1 Holding the slip knot, wrap the yarn from back to front around the hook. This movement is called "yarn over".
   You can wind the yarn over the hook or twist the hook to go under the yarn.
2 Draw the hook backward to pull the yarn through the loop on the hook (the slip knot).
3 You will form a new loop on your hook. You have now made your first chain stitch. Repeat the previous steps to form as many chain stitches as required.

Note: It's crucial to hold the yarn tail firmly to prevent it from spinning around the hook every time you try to yarn over.

Foundation chain
This is the string of chain stitches you have to crochet if you want to make a flat fabric worked in rows. It's the equivalent of casting on when you start knitting.

Note: To help maintain an even foundation chain, keep changing your grip on the crocheted chains, so you are always holding them near the hook.

Turning chain

When crocheting in rows, these are the chain stitches you have to make to bring the hook up to the height of the stitches you are crocheting. Each stitch has a corresponding number of turning chains:
– a row of single crochet: 1 turning chain
– a row of half double crochet: 2 turning chains
– a row of double crochet: 3 turning chains

Note: *Remember to count your stitches now and then to make sure you have the exact number of stitches required in the pattern. When counting stitches, do not count the slip knot or the loop on the hook (this is the working loop). The easiest way to count stitches is to look at the plaited tops.*

Back ridge or back bump of a chain

You can crochet in the chain in different ways. My favorite method for creating a nice, finished bottom edge is to crochet in the back ridge. Each chain consists of three strands of yarn. On the front you can see the two strands you are most familiar with: the top loop and the bottom loop that make up the V. When you turn the chain, you will see a third, hidden loop. This is the 'back bump'. To work in the back ridge of a chain, turn your foundation chain a little, so you can easily reach this back bump.

SLIP STITCH *(abbreviation: slst)*

This stitch has no height and is hardly ever used on its own to make a crochet fabric. Instead, it's generally used to join ends into a circle, join pieces, finish a piece or move across the stitches to another part of the work.

1 Insert the hook through both loops of the next stitch (on the foundation chain: insert in second chain from the hook).
2 Yarn over the hook and draw through both loops at once and the loop on your hook. You have now completed one slip stitch.

Note: *When working slip stitches in the last round or row to finish or embellish a piece, try to work the stitches a little more loosely to avoid puckering the fabric.*

Join a chain ring with a slip stitch (tubular foundation chain)

1 Insert the hook into the first chain. Make sure the chain is not twisted.
2 Yarn over and draw the yarn through the stitch and the loop on your hook. You can now continue working in the round.

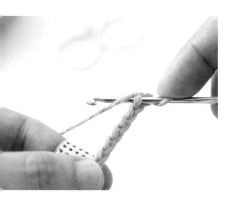

SINGLE CROCHET *(abbreviation: sc)*

The single crochet is THE stitch for working crocheted toys because it's the only one that results in a closed and tight fabric. The single crochet not only works excellently to maintain the shape of the toy, but also avoids that stuffing will show through (as long as we don't stuff it too much).

In rows (flat fabric)

Start from a foundation chain.
1 Insert the hook in the second chain stitch from the hook. Yarn over the hook.
2 Pull the yarn through the chain stitch. Now you have two loops on the hook. Yarn over the hook again.
3 Draw the hook backward to pull the yarn through both loops at once. One loop remains on the hook, and you have completed one single crochet stitch.
4 Insert the hook into the next stitch and continue crocheting into every chain stitch.
5 At the end of a row, make one turning chain and turn the work horizontally to begin the next row. Crochet one single crochet stitch into the next stitch (not counting the turning chain), inserting the hook through both loops of the stitch in the row below. Continue crocheting until the end of the row and repeat.

In a spiral (a tube)

Start from a foundation chain. Make sure your chain isn't twisted and insert the hook in the first chain stitch. Close into a ring by making one slip stitch in the first chain stitch.

1   Continue crocheting one single crochet stitch into each chain stitch until you reach the beginning. Work a single crochet stitch into the first single crochet you made (do not close the round with a slst). This is when the stitch marker comes in handy: place it into the last single crochet stitch you made.

2   Continue working single crochet stitches until you reach the stitch marker. Remove the marker and work a single crochet in this stitch. Replace the marker into the stitch you just made and repeat.

INSERT THE HOOK (PLACEMENT OF STITCHES)

With the exception of chains, for all crochet stitches the hook needs to be inserted into existing stitches. The point of the hook must look down or sideways, so the hook doesn't snag the yarn or the fabric. When picking up stitches, you can insert the hook in three different places: the back loop, the front loop or under both loops.

– BOTH LOOPS: insert the hook under both loops of the stitch in the row or round below. This is the most common way to crochet and the preferred method when the pattern doesn't specify another way.

– FRONT LOOP ONLY (abbreviation FLO): insert the hook under the one loop closest to you.

– BACK LOOP ONLY (abbreviation BLO): insert the hook under the one loop furthest away from you. This leaves the front loop as a horizontal bar. It's used for aesthetic effects or to re-join the yarn.

Difference between V and X single crochet

If you're an experienced crocheter you might have noticed that my stitches look slightly different from what you're accustomed to. Instead of wrapping the yarn over my crochet hook, I wrap it under my crochet hook, that is, I "yarn under". By doing this, I get an X-shaped single crochet stitch instead of a V-shaped single crochet stitch.

Yarn over.

Apart from the different look, there are a few more differences you should know about.

– **Size:** X-shaped single crochet is much tighter, so the result will be smaller. Vice versa, the fabric made using V-shaped single crochet is more fluid/elastic, so the toy will be softer. For example, if I make a circle of 60 stitches using X-shaped single crochet, my circle will be about 3.3 inches / 8.5 cm in diameter. If I make it using V-shaped single crochet, its diameter is about 4 inches / 10 cm.

– **How the stitches seem to turn around:** V-shaped single crochet stitches move a little in each round, so your crochetwork appears to turn to one side. X-shaped single crochet is less likely to do this, which will give nicer results when crocheting jacquard.

– **How the stripe patterns look:** X-shaped single crochet looks like a half double crochet stitch when making stripes in alternating colors.

Yarn under.

Note: *Humboldt Penguin on the left side was made with V-shaped single crochet. Humboldt on the right side was made with X-shaped single crochet.*

HALF DOUBLE CROCHET (abbreviation: hdc)

As its name indicates, this stitch is halfway between a single crochet and a double crochet stitch in height. Being a looser stitch, the fabric made with half double crochet stitch is more fluid and so this stitch is excellent for working toy garments.

In rows (flat fabric)

Start from a foundation chain. The first two chain stitches of the foundation chain are the turning chain for the first row.

1 Yarn over. Insert the hook into the third chain from the hook and yarn over again.
2 Draw the yarn through one loop only. You now have three loops on the hook.
3 Yarn over again and draw through all three loops on the hook.
4 You have completed the first half double crochet stitch.

5 Continue crocheting into every chain stitch.
6 At the end of the row, make two turning chains and turn the work horizontally to begin the next row. Skip the turning chains and crochet one half double crochet stitch, inserting the hook under both loops of the stitch in the row below. Repeat until you reach the end of the row.

Note: *I sometimes work between the stitches when working half double or double crochet in rounds. It creates an open effect that makes for a more elastic fabric. To do this, insert the hook between the stems of the stitches, not under the plaited top. Make sure to count the stitches at the end of your round.*

HALF DOUBLE SLIP STITCH *(abbreviation: hdslst)*

This is an easy stitch to create a dense and stretchy fabric, perfect for ribbing or to make pieces that need a knit-purl look. As the name suggests, it's a mash up of a slip stitch and a half double crochet stitch, You may also find it as Yarn Over Slip Stitch.

In rows (flat fabric)

Start from a foundation chain with any number of chains. Please note that the turning chain doesn't count as a stitch.

1   Yarn over. Insert the hook into the second chain from the hook
2   Yarn over again and pull up a loop. You now have 3 loops on the hook
3   Pull the first loop directly through the second and third loop on the hook. You have completed the first half double slip stitch. Continue crocheting into every chain stitch. At the end of the row, make a turning chain and turn the work horizontally to begin the next row.

From the next row on, you will work in the BACK LOOP ONLY (and will be having one of the largest abbreviations in the history of crochet: BLO hdslst) to create the texture of a faux knit ribbed fabric.

Row 2:
4   Yarn over. Insert the hook into the back loop of the first stitch. Yarn over and pull the first loop directly through the stitch and the second and third loop on the hook. Continue crocheting into every chain stitch till the end of the row. At the end of the row, make a turning chain and turn the work horizontally to begin the next row.

Repeat row 2 until you reach the desire length.

 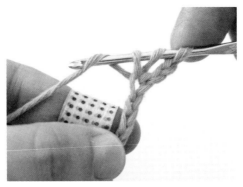 

DOUBLE CROCHET *(abbreviation: dc)*

Probably the best-known crochet stitch to crochet garments and blankets. We only use it sporadically when crocheting toys.

In rows (flat fabric)

Start from a foundation chain. The first three chain stitches of the foundation chain are the turning chain for the first row.

1   Yarn over. Insert the hook into the fourth chain from the hook and yarn over again. Draw the yarn through the loop. You now have three loops on the hook.

2   Yarn over again and draw through the first two loops on the hook.

3   You now have two loops on the hook. Wrap the yarn over the hook one last time and draw it through both loops on the hook.

4   You have now completed one double crochet stitch.

5   Yarn over and insert the hook into the next stitch. Continue crocheting into every chain stitch. At the end of the row, make three turning chains and turn the work horizontally to begin the next row.

6   Skip the turning chains and crochet one double crochet stitch, inserting the hook under both loops of the stitch in the row below. Repeat until you reach the end of the row.

BOBBLE STITCH *(abbreviation: 5-dc-bobble)*

A bobble stitch is a cluster of double crochet stitches worked into one stitch, joined by leaving the last loop of each stitch temporarily on the hook until they are closed together at the end. I use this stitch on many of my toys to make fingers and toes.

1. Yarn over. Insert the hook into the next stitch.
2. Yarn over again and draw the yarn through the stitch. You now have three loops on the hook.
3. Yarn over the hook again and draw it through the first two loops on the hook. You now have one half-closed double crochet stitch, and two loops remaining on the hook.
4. In the same stitch, repeat the preceding steps four times. You now have 5 half-closed double crochet stitches into one stitch.
5. Yarn over and draw through all six loops on the hook at once. You have now completed one 5-dc bobble stitch.

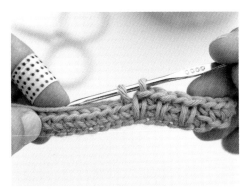  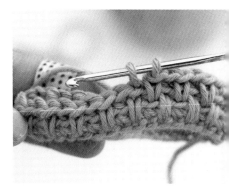

BASKET SPIKE STITCH

This stitch is named for its basket-rattan look. I've only worked it in the round because it doesn't look so neat when crocheted in rows. Alternate one spike single crochet with a regular BLO single crochet to get the desired effect. For this stitch, I use the V-shaped single crochet in order to obtain two straight vertical lines.

Spike single crochet (spike)

Place your hook in the next stitch one round below (into the same place where that stitch was worked). Yarn over and draw up a loop of yarn up to the height of the actual round. Draw the yarn through both loops on your hook.

In a spiral (a tube)

Start from a foundation chain. Make sure your chain isn't twisted and put the hook through the first chain stitch. Close into a ring by making one slip stitch in the first chain. Continue crocheting one single crochet stitch into each chain stitch until you reach the beginning.

1-2 (BLO sc in next st, spike in next st of the previous round) repeat until the end of the round.
3-4 (spike in next st of the previous round, BLO sc in next st) repeat until the end of the round.
Repeat until you have the number of rounds needed.

CRAB STITCH OR REVERSE SINGLE CROCHET

The crab stitch is a stitch that looks like a twisted cording. It creates a rounded edge that's really nice for finishing garments.

It's also known as 'reverse single crochet' because it's worked the same as a single crochet stitch but in the opposite direction. If you're right-handed, crab stitch goes from left to right. And if you are left-handed, from right to left. It may feel a bit awkward at first, but nothing is so complicated that it cannot be achieved with a little practice and patience.

You will work this stitch in a finished piece. Make sure the right side is facing you

1. Chain 1 if you are using the same yarn as you were using in your project or join yarn and chain 1 if you are using a different color.
2. Insert your hook into the stitch to the right of your chain. Yarn over and pull up a loop like you would do for a single crochet stitch, except, as you may notice, the loop will be twisted. You now have two loops on the hook.
3. Yarn over again and pull the yarn through both loops on the hook. You have completed your first crab stitch.
4. Insert the hook into the next stitch to the right, yarn over and pull up a loop. Yarn over and pull through both loops on the hook.
5. Continue crocheting until you reach the end or, if you are working an edging that starts and ends in the same place, continue till you reach the stitch you started in. Slip stitch into that stitch (the same stitch you started in or the last one).

INCREASES AND DECREASES

Increases and decreases are used for shaping any crochet garment or object.

Increase *(abbreviation: inc)*

Increasing in crochet is achieved by working two or more stitches where there would normally be one stitch.
1 Work a stitch into the next stitch of the previous row or round.
2 Insert your hook in exactly the same stitch and pull up a loop.
3 Work a second stitch.

Decrease *(abbreviation: dec)*

Decreasing is achieved by crocheting two or more stitches together. There are a couple of methods, but for my toys I always use the "traditional decrease" because it's the method I learned first and it comes naturally to me. Nowadays, it's become less popular because it can leave a small gap if not tightened properly.
1-2 Work two incomplete stitches in two adjacent stitches on the previous round or row.
3 Yarn over.
4 Pull the loop through all three loops on the hook.

Working in spirals

Increasing stitches from the center out is a technique used to make round pieces, such as hats and doilies. When crocheting in rounds, we traditionally close each round with a slip stitch. This technique, despite generating perfect circles, leaves a continuous mark, something like a scar, and it's not pretty at all on a cute toy.
To avoid this mark, we usually choose to crochet in spirals, that is, without joining the rounds.

When working in continuous spirals, it's highly recommended to use a stitch marker. This tool will show you where a new round begins and the previous one ended. You can choose to place it at the end or the beginning of each round (be consistent in what you choose). After crocheting the round, you should end up right above your stitch marker. Move it at the beginning or the end of each round to keep track of where you are.

MAGIC RING

This is, almost without a doubt, the best way to start crocheting in the round. You start by working the required number of stitches on an adjustable loop and then pull the loop tight until the stitches are closed in a ring.
There are several techniques to start the magic ring, and all of them may seem a bit scary at first. Practice and don't worry if it appears impossible during the first attempts. I can assure you that once you've finished your first toy, you will have mastered this technique. And you'll love it!

1   Start with the yarn crossed to form a circle, as if you were to start a slip knot.

2-3 Holding the loop tight between your thumb and index finger, insert the hook in the middle of the circle and draw up a loop.

4   Keep holding the ring tight (this is crucial!) and yarn over again above the circle. Pull the yarn through the loop on your hook to make a chain stitch. This chain stitch will secure the ring.

5-6 Insert the hook again into the circle and underneath the tail (they look like two strands crossed). Yarn over the hook and draw up a loop.

7   Yarn over again above the circle. Draw the loop through both loops on the hook. You've now made your first single crochet stitch in the ring.

8   Make as many stitches as required in the pattern. Grab the yarn tail and pull to draw the center of the ring tightly closed. Don't be afraid to pull it really tight.

9   You can opt to join the circle with a slip stitch, but this is not necessary. It's the only point where I myself join the rounds.

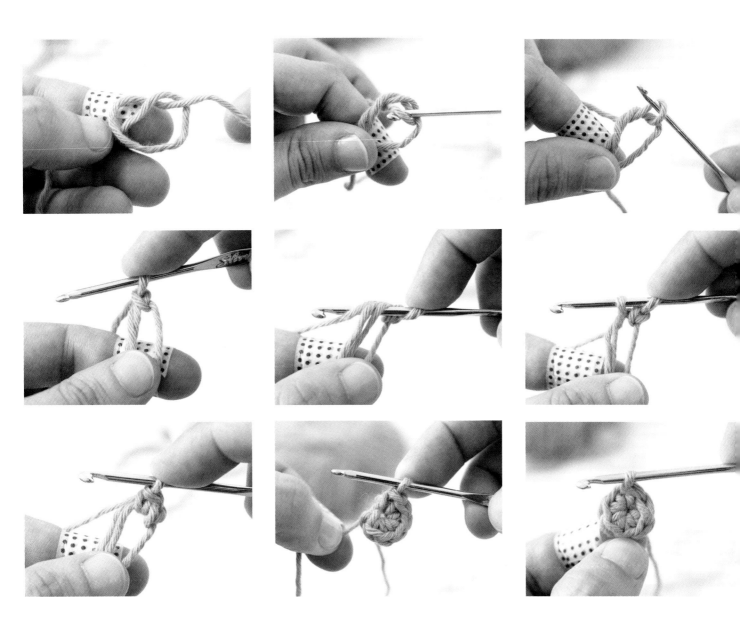

CROCHETING AROUND A FOUNDATION CHAIN

When you want to start an oval piece instead of a circle, you can start by working around a foundation chain. It's the traditional method to start rugs or bags and, in case of toys, we'll be using this technique for crocheting snouts, ears and the body of some characters.

1   Work a foundation chain with as many stitches as required. Start in the second chain from the hook and make a single crochet stitch (sometimes, the pattern may require an increase stitch).

Continue crocheting single crochet stitches into each chain stitch.

2   The last stitch is usually an increase stitch, so we can turn the work and continue working on the other side of the foundation chain.

3-4   Turn your work upside down to work into the underside of the stitches. Notice that only one loop is available.

5   Continue crocheting into each loop across. Your last single crochet stitch should be next to the first stitch you made. It can also be an increase stitch (depending on the pattern).

6   You can now continue working in spirals.

CHANGING COLOR AND JOINING YARN

Use this technique when you want to switch from one color to the next or join yarn because you ran out of the one you were crocheting with.

1. Work in the previous color (or yarn) until two loops of the last stitch remain on the hook.
2. Use the new color (or yarn) to complete the stitch.
   Continue working with the new color (or yarn) as before. Try not to cut off any yarn tails that will be needed later on. I knot both yarns, to make sure the stitch stays tight.

Note: *If you are working stripes of different colors in rows, make the color change in the last stitch of the previous row.*

TAPESTRY CROCHET IN BOTH LOOPS

TAPESTRY CROCHET IN FLO

TAPESTRY CROCHET IN BLO

JACQUARD AND TAPESTRY

These two funny words come from other textile worlds, knitting and weaving, but crocheters managed to adapt these color change techniques to crochet. They are used to create motifs and patterns with two or more colors, much like drawing with different yarn colors.
It's common to work these motifs by following a diagram that shows you the color for each stitch. Using a diagram makes it easier to count stitches.

The difference between the two techniques is how the different strands of color are carried through the work.

When working **jacquard**, we leave the yarn we don't use behind the work. When it's time to use it again, you pick up the yarn and carry it across the back (inside) of your work before making the next color change.
When the pattern indicates to make a color change, it's really important to remember that the change must always be started one stitch earlier. Crochet the number of stitches as indicated by the pattern/diagram. Taking into account that the color change always starts a stitch before, take the strand of the color that you want to use and carry it from behind to the place where you want to change color. The strands that remain inside your crochetwork between color changes must be loose enough so that the fabric doesn't pucker.

Note: *When working jacquard with color changes that are widely spread, I like to cut the inside strands and tie them together. In fact, it is recommended if the color change causes your thread to cross the crochetwork and make a web that doesn't allow you to stuff properly. If you don't want to cut your yarn, you can also use the technique of picking up the loose strand every couple of stitches.*

When working the **tapestry technique,** you carry the yarn strand along within the stitches (on top of the V) while continuing to crochet with the other color. This means that every time we make a stitch, we'll be wrapping the strand(s) of the other yarn color(s) that we aren't using. This apparently small difference with the jacquard technique will result in a significantly different fabric, especially on the backside (or "wrong" side): it results in a piece of fabric that resembles a tapestry (hence the name!) and has the great advantage that there are no loose threads on either side. Therefore, it's great to crochet garments or accessories where we want the fabric to look nice on both sides. However, the small disadvantage I do see is that, unless you carry the threads throughout the entire work, the place where you crochet using this technique results in a rather thick fabric, and the threads of the "hidden" colors can be seen between the stitches.

Note: If you want straight vertical lines using the tapestry technique with single crochet stitches, you may want to crochet FLO or BLO (sample on page 35).

FASTENING OFF

When you finish your work and want to fasten off the yarn permanently, cut the yarn about 2 inches / 5 cm away from the last stitch. Draw the end through the loop on the hook.
If you are going to sew the piece, you may have to cut the yarn much longer, depending on how many stitches you'll have to sew. If you are not going to sew this piece, or if you have finished the last round of a stuffed piece, you may want to weave in the yarn end.

Weave in the yarn end on a flat fabric

Thread the yarn end into a tapestry needle. With the wrong side facing, weave the end into a single row or several stitches, wrapping the yarn end into the loops at the bottom of the rows. You can also pass the yarn through the loops on the side. Cut the remaining tail.

Weave in the yarn end on a stuffed piece

1-2 Finish the last round of decreases and fasten off, leaving a long tail of 6 inches / 15 cm. Thread the yarn tail into a tapestry needle and, from back to front, weave it through the front loop of each remaining stitch.

3 Pull the yarn tail tight to close. Weave it through one or two more stitches to secure the tail. Trim the excess yarn and hide it into the piece with the help of your crochet hook.

EMBROIDERY

Embroidery remains a pending subject for me. I only know – more or less – how to make one embroidery stitch I learned as a child to hand-sew doll dresses: the **backstitch**. It creates a nice line made up of straight stitches.

1 Thread your tapestry needle. Insert the needle from behind your work and make a single straight stitch the same length as your single crochet stitch. I like to use the gaps between the stitches to insert and pass the tapestry needle through.

2 Continue along, as many times as you need, coming up one space ahead and bringing your needle back down into the same hole at the end of the last stitch you've made.

JOINING PARTS (SEWING)

I'm one of many crocheters who would happily pay someone to do the sewing part for me. But, as there are no volunteers (yet), we better practice a simple and satisfactory method. If you're having doubts about where to place the parts, you can pin them to see how they look and adjust if necessary. If possible, use the leftover yarn tail from where you fastened off.

Joining open pieces

Use this technique to sew snouts, cheeks, beaks, horns, etc., to an open and unstuffed piece, like a head. Thread the tapestry needle and position the piece. Use pins if you need them! If you are sewing a snout or a beak on a face, I recommend you position it on the opposite side of where your stitch marker is located, for aesthetic reasons. This way your color changes will be at the back of your toy. Make the first stitch, inserting the needle from front to back (inside). Using backstitching, sew passing under both loops of each stitch from the final round of the piece to be attached. Go from back to front and front to back. If the piece has 30 stitches, you'll have to make 30 backstitches. Before getting to the end, remember to stuff the piece. I try not to stuff the pieces until the very end, to avoid the filling getting entangled in the stitches.

Joining an open end piece with a closed piece

I'll explain how to sew an open piece (with or without stuffing) onto a finished and closed part without closing the opening first. Thread the tapestry needle. Place the pieces on top of each other and try to line up the stitches of one piece with the other, if possible. Insert the needle through one loop of the closed (and stuffed) piece (for example the body). Now pass the needle under both loops of the stitch from the piece to be sewn. Sew around the whole piece and fasten off. Weave in the yarn tail.

 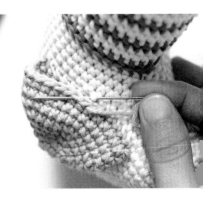

READING A PATTERN

Crochet has its own lingo and, like all lingos, its own peculiarities. The crochet terminology not only differs between countries, it even has its local variations in the same country. The table below is a brief guide to the most commonly used stitch terms and their crochet symbols. In this book, I use US terms.

US	UK	LATIN AMERICA	SPAIN	SYMBOL
stitch (st)	stitch (st)	punto (p/pt)	punto (p/pt)	
chain (ch)	chain (ch)	cadena (c/cad)	cadeneta (c/cad)	⬯
slip stitch (slst)	slip stitch (slst)	punto corrido / pasado (pc/pp)	punto raso / enano (pr/pe)	⬮
single crochet (sc)	double crochet (dc)	medio punto (mp)	punto bajo (pb)	✕
half double crochet (hdc)	half treble crochet (htc)	media vareta (mv/pmv)	punto (alto) medio (pm)	T
double crochet (dc)	treble crochet (tr)	vareta (v/pv)	punto alto (pa)	Ŧ
bobble stitch	bobble stitch	punto mota / piña	punto piña	⊕
increase (inc)	increase (inc)	aumento (aum)	aumento (aum)	V̄
decrease (dec)	decrease (dec)	disminución (dism)	disminución (dism)	Ā
round (Rnd)	round (Rnd)	ronda (r)	ronda (r)	
ring	ring	anillo	anillo	

PARENTHESES AND BRACKETS

In this book, I use parentheses (rounded brackets) to indicate the instructions that should be repeated across the round or row a required number of times. The number within square brackets at the end of each line shows the total number of stitches you should have in the previous round.

For example: **Rnd 3:** (sc in next st, inc in next st) repeat 6 times [18]

Rnd 3 indicates in which round you are. The instructions inside the parentheses are the stitches you have to work 6 times through the round. 18 is the total number of stitches you should have at the end.

When directions for one round must be repeated through several rounds, you will read "Rnd 10 – 20", which indicates that you have to follow the same instructions from round 10 up to (and including) round 20.

Lucas Red Fox

When Lucas was a little fox, instead of playing hide and seek with his friends, he would stay inside, devouring every mystery and detective book he could find. With time, he found himself loving all kinds of books. Every time Lucas got hold of a new title, he stared at the cover, studied every detail, touched the paper, smelled the ink... And if he discovered drawings, engravings or pictures inside, he would jump around the house with joy. So, when he grew up, he started working in a small-scale printing house surrounded by the smell of ink and a thousand types of paper. He now creates books and is quite awesome at making a story look spectacular. In fact, he's quite awesome at all he does, except making bubbles with gum. He blames his large snout.

 GALLERY: Scan or visit *www.amigurumi.com/4101* to share pictures and find inspiration.

 SKILL LEVEL *

Size:
13.5 inches / 34 cm tall when made with the indicated yarn (ears included)

Materials:
– Worsted weight yarn in
· red
· off-white
· blue
· white
· black (leftover)
· pastel pink (leftover)
– Size C-2 / 2.75 mm crochet hook
– Black safety eyes (10 mm)
– Tapestry needle
– Fiberfill

Skills needed: magic ring *(page 32)*, changing color at the beginning of a round *(page 35)*, embroidery *(page 38)*, joining parts *(page 39)*, dividing the body in two parts *(explained in pattern)*

Note: The head and body are worked in one piece.

CHEEKS

(make 2, in pastel pink)
Rnd 1: start 8 sc in a magic ring [8]
Slst in next st. Fasten off, leaving a long tail for sewing.

SNOUT

(start in black)
Rnd 1: start 6 sc in a magic ring [6]
Rnd 2: inc in all 6 st [12]
Rnd 3 – 6: sc in all 12 st [12]
Change to off-white yarn.
Rnd 7: (sc in next st, inc in next st) repeat 6 times [18]
Rnd 8 – 10: sc in all 18 st [18]
Change to red yarn.
Rnd 11: sc in next 8 st, inc in next 2 st, sc in next 8 st [20]
Rnd 12: sc in all 20 st [20]
Fasten off, leaving a long tail for sewing. Embroider the mouth with black yarn. Stuff the snout with fiberfill.

HEAD AND BODY

(start in red)
Rnd 1: start 6 sc in a magic ring [6]
Rnd 2: inc in all 6 st [12]
Rnd 3: (sc in next st, inc in next st) repeat 6 times [18]
Rnd 4: (sc in next st, inc in next st) repeat 9 times [27]
Rnd 5: (sc in next 2 st, inc in next st) repeat 9 times [36]
Rnd 6: (sc in next 3 st, inc in next st) repeat 9 times [45]
Rnd 7: (sc in next 4 st, inc in next st) repeat 9 times [54]
Rnd 8: (sc in next 8 st, inc in next st) repeat 6 times [60]
Rnd 9 – 21: sc in all 60 st [60]
Rnd 22: (sc in next 3 st, dec) repeat 12 times [48]
Rnd 23: (sc in next 2 st, dec) repeat 12 times [36]
Sew the snout between rounds 14 and 20. The snout must be placed on the opposite side of the start of the round. Insert the safety eyes between rounds 16 and 17, about 3 stitches away from

44

the snout. Sew the cheeks below the safety eyes.

Rnd 24: (sc in next 4 st, dec) repeat 6 times [30]

Rnd 25: (sc in next st, dec) repeat 10 times [20]

Rnd 26: sc in all 20 st [20]

Stuff the head firmly. Continue in a stripe pattern, changing color every round, alternating white and blue yarn.

Rnd 27: (sc in next st, inc in next st) repeat 10 times [30]

Rnd 28 – 31: sc in all 30 st [30]

Rnd 32: (sc in next 4 st, inc in next st) repeat 6 times [36]

Rnd 33 – 37: sc in all 36 st [36]

Rnd 38: (sc in next 8 st, inc in next st) repeat 4 times [40]

Rnd 39: sc in all 40 st [40]

Change to red yarn.

Rnd 40: BLO sc in all 40 st [40]

Rnd 41 – 48: sc in all 40 st [40]

Do not fasten off.

LEGS

To make the legs, divide the work identifying 4 stitches for the front central space between the legs, 4 stitches for the back and 16 stitches for each leg (you may find it useful to use stitch markers). If the legs don't line up nicely with the head, crochet a few more sc on the body or undo them. Join the marked stitch for the leg on the back side to the marked stitch on the front side, working a single crochet stitch (this sc will be the first stitch of the leg). Now the stitches of the first leg are joined in the round. Continue working the first leg:

Rnd 49 – 70: sc in all 16 st [16]

Stuff the body and leg firmly.

Rnd 71: (sc in next 2 st, dec) repeat 4 times [12]

Rnd 72: dec 6 times [6]

Fasten off, leaving a long tail. Using a tapestry needle, weave the yarn tail through the front loop of each remaining stitch and pull tight to close. Weave in the yarn end.

SECOND LEG

Rejoin the red yarn in the fifth unworked stitch at the back of round 48. This is where we start the first stitch of the second leg. Leave a long starting yarn tail.

Rnd 49: sc in next 16 st. When you reach the 16th st of the leg, sc in first st to join the round [16]

Rnd 50 – 72: repeat the pattern for the first leg.

Stuff the second leg and add more stuffing to the body if needed. Using a tapestry needle and the starting yarn tail, sew the 4 stitches between the legs closed.

ARMS

(make 2, start in red)

Rnd 1: start 6 sc in a magic ring [6]

Rnd 2: inc in all 6 st [12]

Rnd 3 – 4: sc in all 12 st [12]

Rnd 5: sc in next st, 5-dc-bobble in next st, sc in next 10 st [12]

Rnd 6 – 16: sc in all 12 st [12]

Continue in a stripe pattern, changing color every round, alternating white and blue yarn.

Rnd 17 – 21: sc in all 12 st [12]

Rnd 22: (sc in next st, dec) repeat 4 times [8]

Fasten off, leaving a long tail for sewing. Stuff with fiberfill. Sew the arms to both sides between rounds 28 and 29.

TAIL

(start in off-white)

Rnd 1: start 6 sc in a magic ring [6]

Rnd 2: inc in all 6 st [12]

Rnd 3: (sc in next st, inc in next st) repeat 6 times [18]

Rnd 4: sc in all 18 st [18]

Rnd 5: (sc in next 2 st, inc in next st) repeat 6 times [24]

Rnd 6: sc in all 24 st [24]

Rnd 7: (sc in next 5 st, inc in next st) repeat 4 times [28]

Rnd 8: sc in all 28 st [28]

Rnd 9: (sc in next 6 st, inc in next st) repeat 4 times [32]

Rnd 10: sc in all 32 st [32]

Change to red yarn.

Rnd 11 – 16: sc in all 32 st [32]
Rnd 17: (sc in next 6 st, dec) repeat 4 times [28]
Rnd 18 – 19: sc in all 28 st [28]
Rnd 20: (sc in next 5 st, dec) repeat 4 times [24]
Rnd 21 – 22: sc in all 24 st [24]
Rnd 23: (sc in next 4 st, dec) repeat 4 times [20]
Rnd 24 – 25: sc in all 20 st [20]

Rnd 26: (sc in next 3 st, dec) repeat 4 times [16]
Rnd 27 – 28: sc in all 16 st [16]
Rnd 29: (sc in next 2 st, dec) repeat 4 times [12]
Rnd 30: sc in all 12 st [12]
Fasten off, leaving a long tail for sewing. Stuff with fiberfill, but stuff less at the top. Sew the tail to the back, centered over rounds 43 and 44.

EARS

(make 2, in red)
Rnd 1: start 6 sc in a magic ring [6]
Rnd 2: inc in all 6 st [12]
Rnd 3: sc in all 12 st [12]
Rnd 4: (sc in next 3 st, inc in next st) repeat 3 times [15]
Rnd 5 – 7: sc in all 15 st [15]
Rnd 8: (sc in next 4 st, inc in next st) repeat 3 times [18]
Rnd 9 – 11: sc in all 18 st [18]
Rnd 12: (sc in next 5 st, inc in next st) repeat 3 times [21]
Rnd 13 – 15: sc in all 21 st [21]
Fasten off, leaving a long tail for sewing. The ears do not need to be stuffed. Embroider off-white stripes on the inside of the ear. Flatten the ears before sewing them to the head.

Gilbert Rabbit

Gilbert is a poet. He loves wandering in the fields, listening to the wind blowing through the tall grass, the buzz of the bees, watching the tiny bright speckles of light that sneak through the leafy canopy… and writing his findings down in thousands of notebooks that he leaves scattered around his home. He's not the most organized or tidy type of person. But he is a great poet. In his spare time, he works as an editor in a publishing house specialized in knitting and crochet patterns. Gilbert's exceptional attention to detail allows him to find every tiny mistake in a sea of digits, sentences, and paragraphs. And from time to time, he throws in a tiny poetic metaphor so that the stitches don't feel so boring.

GALLERY: Scan or visit *www.amigurumi.com/4102* to share pictures and find inspiration.

SKILL LEVEL * *

Size:
15 inches / 38 cm tall when made with the indicated yarn (ears included)

Materials:
– Worsted weight yarn in
· slate gray
· off-white
· yellow
· black (leftover)
· pastel pink
· pale pink
· cream
· graphite
· beige
– Size C-2 / 2.75 mm crochet hook
– Black safety eyes (10 mm)
– Tapestry needle
– Fiberfill

Skills needed: magic ring *(page 32)*, changing color at the beginning of a round *(page 35)*, changing color mid-round *(page 35)*, dividing the body in two parts *(page 47)*, joining parts *(page 39)*, embroidery *(page 38)*

Note: The head and body are worked in one piece.

CHEEKS

(make 2, in pastel pink)
Rnd 1: start 8 sc in a magic ring [8]
Slst in next st. Fasten off, leaving a long tail for sewing.

SNOUT

(in off-white)
Rnd 1: start 6 sc in a magic ring [6]
Rnd 2: inc in all 6 st [12]
Rnd 3: (sc in next st, inc in next st) repeat 6 times [18]
Rnd 4: sc in all 18 st [18]
Fasten off, leaving a long tail for sewing. Embroider the nose and mouth with black yarn.

HEAD AND BODY

(start in slate gray)
Rnd 1: start 6 sc in a magic ring [6]
Rnd 2: inc in all 6 st [12]

Rnd 3: (sc in next st, inc in next st) repeat 6 times [18]
Rnd 4: (sc in next 2 st, inc in next st) repeat 6 times [24]
Rnd 5: (sc in next 3 st, inc in next st) repeat 6 times [30]
Rnd 6: (sc in next 4 st, inc in next st) repeat 6 times [36]
Rnd 7: (sc in next 5 st, inc in next st) repeat 6 times [42]
Rnd 8: (sc in next 6 st, inc in next st) repeat 6 times [48]
Rnd 9: (sc in next 7 st, inc in next st) repeat 6 times [54]
Rnd 10: (sc in next 8 st, inc in next st) repeat 6 times [60]
Rnd 11 – 22: sc in all 60 st [60]
Rnd 23: (sc in next 3 st, dec) repeat 12 times [48]
Rnd 24: (sc in next 2 st, dec) repeat 12 times [36]
Sew the snout between rounds 14 and 19. The snout must be placed on the opposite side of the start of the round. Stuff the snout with fiberfill before closing the seam. Insert the safety eyes between rounds 16 and 17, about 3 stitches away from the snout. Sew the cheeks below the safety eyes. Embroider short beige lines on the forehead.
Rnd 25: (sc in next 4 st, dec) repeat 6 times [30]

Rnd 26: (sc in next st, dec) repeat 10 times [20]
Rnd 27: sc in all 20 st [20]
Stuff the head firmly. Change to off-white yarn.
Rnd 28: (sc in next st, inc in next st) repeat 10 times [30]
Continue working in a stripe pattern, alternating 2 rounds in yellow and 1 round in off-white yarn.
Rnd 29 – 32: sc in all 30 st [30]
Rnd 33: (sc in next 4 st, inc in next st) repeat 6 times [36]
Rnd 34 – 38: sc in all 36 st [36]
Rnd 39: (sc in next 8 st, inc in next st) repeat 4 times [40]
Rnd 40: sc in all 40 st [40]
Change to slate gray yarn.
Rnd 41: BLO sc in all 40 st [40]
Rnd 42 – 49: sc in all 40 st [40]
Do not fasten off.

LEGS

To make the legs, divide the work identifying 4 stitches for the front central space between the legs, 4 stitches for the back and 16 stitches for each leg (you may find it useful to use stitch markers). If the legs don't line up nicely with the head, crochet a few more sc on the body or undo them. Join the marked stitch for the leg on the back side to the marked stitch on the front side, working a single crochet stitch (this sc will be the first stitch of the leg). Now the stitches of the first leg are joined in the round. Continue working the first leg:
Rnd 50 – 71: sc in all 16 st [16]
Stuff the body and leg firmly.
Rnd 72: (sc in next 2 st, dec) repeat 4 times [12]
Rnd 73: dec 6 times [6]
Fasten off, leaving a long tail. Using a tapestry needle, weave the yarn tail through the front loop of each remaining stitch and pull tight to close. Weave in the yarn end.

SECOND LEG
Rejoin the slate gray yarn in the fifth unworked stitch at the back of round 49. This is where we start the first stitch of the second leg. Leave a long starting yarn tail.
Rnd 50: sc in next 16 st. When you reach the 16th st of the leg, sc in first st to join the round [16]
Rnd 51 – 73: repeat the pattern for the first leg. Stuff the second leg and add more stuffing to the body if needed. Using a tapestry needle and the starting yarn tail, sew the 4 stitches between the legs closed.

ARMS

(make 2, start in slate gray)
Rnd 1: start 6 sc in a magic ring [6]
Rnd 2: inc in all 6 st [12]
Rnd 3 – 4: sc in all 12 st [12]
Rnd 5: sc in next st, 5-dc-bobble in next st, sc in next 10 st [12]
Rnd 6 – 16: sc in all 12 st [12]
Change to off-white yarn. Continue in a stripe pattern, changing color every round, alternating 1 round in off-white yarn and 2 rounds in yellow yarn.
Rnd 17 – 21: sc in all 12 st [12]
Rnd 22: (sc in next st, dec) repeat 4 times [8]
Fasten off, leaving a long tail for sewing. Stuff with fiberfill. Sew the arms to both sides between rounds 29 and 30.

EARS

(make 2, start in slate gray)

Note: The ears are created with the jacquard technique. Alternatively, you can crochet the ears in a single color and make a separate inner ear by using the pattern of Ramona cow's inner ear on page 100.

Rnd 1: start 5 sc in a magic ring [5]

Rnd 2: inc in all 5 st [10]

Rnd 3: (sc in next st, inc in next st) repeat 5 times [15]

Continue working with alternating yarns (slate gray and beige). The color you work with is indicated before each part.

Rnd 4: *(slate gray)* sc in next 3 st, *(beige)* sc in next 2 st, *(slate gray)* sc in next 10 st [15]

Rnd 5 – 20: *(slate gray)* sc in next 2 st, *(beige)* sc in next 4 st, *(slate gray)* sc in next 9 st [15]

Continue in slate gray yarn.

Rnd 21: sc in all 15 st [15]

Fasten off, leaving a long tail for sewing. Do not stuff. Flatten and pinch the ears and sew them on top of the head.

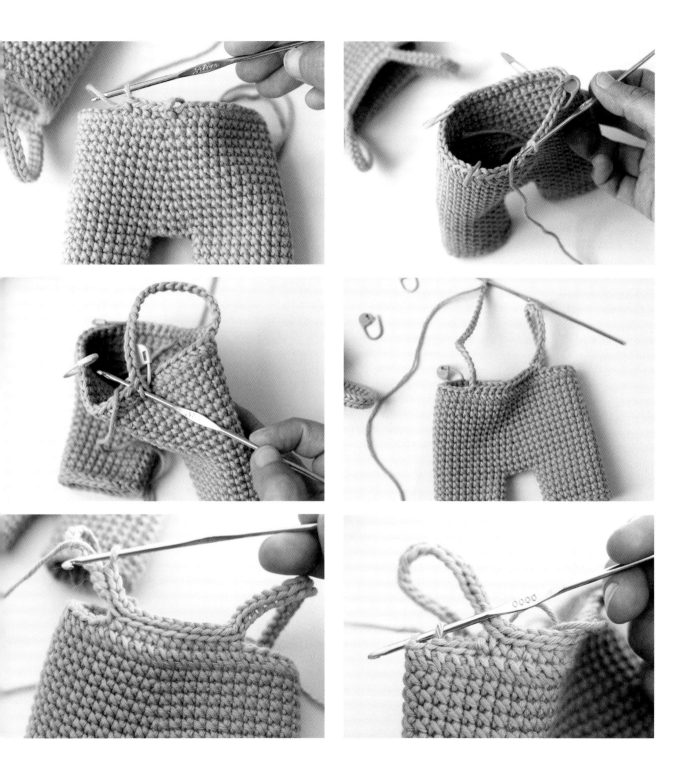

OVERALLS

(start in cream)

Ch 46. Make sure your chain isn't twisted. Insert the hook in the first chain stitch and join the foundation chain with a slst. Continue working in a spiral.

Work in a stripe pattern, changing color every round, alternating cream and graphite gray yarn.

Rnd 1 – 2: sc in all 46 st [46]
Rnd 3: (sc in next 22 st, inc in next st) repeat 2 times [48]
Rnd 4 – 5: sc in all 48 st [48]
Rnd 6: (sc in next 23 st, inc in next st) repeat 2 times [50]
Rnd 7 – 8: sc in all 50 st [50]
Rnd 9: (sc in next 24 st, inc in next st) repeat 2 times [52]
Rnd 10 – 12: sc in all 52 st [52]
Do not fasten off.

OVERALL LEGS

To make the overall legs, divide the work identifying 4 stitches for the central space between the legs, 4 stitches for the back and 22 stitches for each overall leg (you may find it useful to use stitch markers). Join the marked stitch for the overall leg on the back side to the marked stitch on the front side, working a single crochet stitch (this sc will be the first stitch of the next round). Now the stitches of the first overall leg are joined in the round. Continue working the first overall leg in a stripe pattern:

Rnd 13 – 19: sc in all 22 st [22]
Rnd 20: slst in all 22 st [22]
Fasten off and weave in the yarn ends.

SECOND OVERALL LEG

Rejoin the cream yarn in the fifth unworked stitch at the back of round 12. This is where we start the first stitch of the second overall leg. Leave a long starting yarn tail.

Rnd 13: sc in next 22 st. When you reach the 22nd st of the leg, sc in first st to join the round [22]
Rnd 14 – 20: repeat the pattern for the first overall leg. Fasten off and weave in the yarn ends. Using a tapestry needle and the starting yarn tail, sew the 4 stitches between the overall legs closed.

OVERALL WAISTBAND AND STRAPS
(in pastel pink)

Identify the center stitch in round 1 at the back of the overall and join pastel pink yarn in this stitch. Crochet the waistband.

Rnd 1: sc in all 46 st [46]
Continue with the shoulder straps.

Mark stitches 6, 18, 29 and 41 with stitch markers. These 4 stitch markers show where to start or join the straps.

Rnd 2: sc in next 6 st, ch 22, skip next 11 st on the waistband, sc in next marked stitch on the waist-band, sc in next 11 st on the waistband, ch 22, skip next 11 st on the waistband, sc in next marked stitch at the back of the waistband, sc in next 5 st on the waistband [24 + 44 ch]

Rnd 3: BLO slst in next 6 st until you reach the shoulder strap, slst in next 22 st on the shoulder strap, BLO slst in next 12 st on the waistband, slst in next 22 st on the second shoulder strap, BLO slst in next 6 st on the waistband [48]

Next, work around each armhole. For the left armhole, join pastel pink yarn at the back, next to the right strap. BLO slst in next 11 st, slst in next 22 ch. Fasten off and weave in the yarn ends. Repeat for the right armhole, joining pastel pink yarn at the front, next to the left strap.

Make a 1.2" / 3 cm pompon in pale pink yarn and sew it to the back of the overalls.

Olivia Rosemary Mouse

Olivia Rosemary got her middle name from her uncle, "Romero Mouse" (Rosemary in Spanish), and she loves it. Her mother's fascination with Olivia Flaversham, the little mouse in "The Great Mouse Detective", probably got her her first name. Everyone agrees that rosemary and olive are perfect together (especially if you add garlic and potatoes to the combo). Ok, we suppose her mom was simply thinking of dinner when Olivia was born. But, apart from her name origin, Olivia thinks that she does look a lot like Olivia F., and - perhaps influenced by Lucas red fox - she loves mysteries and detective stories so much that she decided she wants to be a private detective. She read all Arthur Conan Doyle books and, of course, started reading the Enola Holmes mysteries...

GALLERY: Scan or visit *www.amigurumi.com/4103* to share pictures and find inspiration.

SKILL LEVEL * *

Size:
12 inches / 30 cm tall when made with the indicated yarn (ears included)

Materials:
– Worsted weight yarn in
  · taupe brown
  · beige
  · pale pink
  · pastel pink (leftover)
  · graphite gray
  · pastel mint
  · petrol blue
– Fingering or light sport weight yarn in
  · off-white
– Size C-2 / 2.75 mm crochet hook
– Size B-1 / 2.25 mm crochet hook
– Black safety eyes (10 mm)
– Tapestry needle
– Fiberfill

Skills needed: magic ring *(page 32)*, changing color mid-round *(page 35)*, dividing the body in two parts *(page 47)*, working tapestry crochet *(page 36)*, joining parts *(page 39)*, embroidery *(page 38)*

Note: *The head and body are worked in one piece.*

Note: *Use a size C-2 / 2.75 mm crochet hook, unless otherwise noted.*

CHEEKS

(make 2, in pastel pink)
Rnd 1: start 6 sc in a magic ring [6]
Rnd 2: inc in all 6 st [12]
Slst in next st. Fasten off, leaving a long tail for sewing.

SNOUT

(in beige)
Rnd 1: start 6 sc in a magic ring [6]
Rnd 2: (sc in next st, inc in next st) repeat 3 times [9]
Rnd 3: sc in all 9 st [9]
Rnd 4: (sc in next 2 st, inc in next st) repeat 3 times [12]
Rnd 5: sc in all 12 st [12]
Fasten off, leaving a long tail for sewing. Embroider the nose and mouth with graphite gray yarn.

HEAD AND BODY

(in taupe brown)
Rnd 1: start 6 sc in a magic ring [6]
Rnd 2: inc in all 6 st [12]
Rnd 3: (sc in next st, inc in next st) repeat 6 times [18]
Rnd 4: (sc in next 2 st, inc in next st) repeat 6 times [24]
Rnd 5: (sc in next 3 st, inc in next st) repeat 6 times [30]
Rnd 6: (sc in next 4 st, inc in next st) repeat 6 times [36]
Rnd 7: (sc in next 5 st, inc in next st) repeat 6 times [42]
Rnd 8: (sc in next 6 st, inc in next st) repeat 6 times [48]
Rnd 9: (sc in next 7 st, inc in next st) repeat 6 times [54]
Rnd 10 – 20: sc in all 54 st [54]
Rnd 21: (sc in next 7 st, dec) repeat 6 times [48]
Rnd 22: (sc in next 2 st, dec) repeat 12 times [36]

Sew the snout between rounds 14 and 18. The snout must be placed on the opposite side of the start of the round. Stuff the snout with fiberfill before closing the seam. Insert the safety eyes between rounds 15 and 16, about 3 stitches away from the snout. Sew the cheeks below the safety eyes.

Rnd 23: (sc in next 4 st, dec) repeat 6 times [30]
Rnd 24: (sc in next 3 st, dec) repeat 6 times [24]
Rnd 25: (sc in next 2 st, dec) repeat 6 times [18]
Rnd 26: sc in all 18 st [18]
Stuff the head firmly.
Rnd 27: (sc in next st, inc in next st) repeat 9 times [27]
Rnd 28: sc in all 27 st [27]
Rnd 29: (sc in next 2 st, inc in next st) repeat 9 times [36]
Rnd 30 – 42: sc in all 36 st [36]
Do not fasten off.

LEGS

To make the legs, divide the work identifying 3 stitches for the front central space between the legs, 3 stitches for the back and 15 stitches for each leg (you may find it useful to use stitch markers). If the legs don't line up nicely with the head, crochet a few more sc on the body or undo them. Join the marked stitch for the leg on the back side to the marked stitch on the front side, working a single crochet stitch (this sc will be the first stitch of the leg). Now the stitches of the first leg are joined in the round. Continue working the first leg:
Rnd 43 – 60: sc in all 15 st [15]
Stuff the body and leg firmly.
Rnd 61: (sc in next st, dec) repeat 5 times [10]
Rnd 62: dec 5 times [5]
Fasten off, leaving a long tail. Using a tapestry needle, weave the yarn tail through the front loop of each remaining stitch and pull tight to close. Weave in the yarn end.

SECOND LEG
Rejoin the taupe brown yarn in the fourth un-worked stitch at the back of round 42. This is where we start the first stitch of the second leg. Leave a long starting yarn tail.
Rnd 43: sc in next 15 st. When you reach the 15th st of the leg, sc in first stitch to join the round [15]
Rnd 44 – 62: repeat the pattern for the first leg. Stuff the second leg and add more stuffing to the body if needed. Using a tapestry needle and the starting yarn tail, sew the 3 stitches between the legs closed.

ARMS

(make 2, in taupe brown)
Rnd 1: start 5 sc in a magic ring [5]
Rnd 2: inc in all 5 st [10]
Rnd 3 – 20: sc in all 10 st [10]
Rnd 21: (sc in next 3 st, dec) repeat 2 times [8]
Fasten off, leaving a long tail for sewing. Stuff with fiberfill. Sew the arms to both sides between rounds 28 and 29.

EARS

(make 2)
The ears are made by joining 2 circles.

INNER CIRCLE
(in pale pink)
Rnd 1: start 8 sc in a magic ring [8]
Rnd 2: inc in all 8 st [16]
Rnd 3: (sc in next st, inc in next st) repeat 8 times [24]
Rnd 4: (sc in next 2 st, inc in next st) repeat 8 times [32]
Rnd 5: (sc in next 3 st, inc in next st) repeat 8 times [40]
Fasten off and weave in the yarn end. Set aside.

OUTER CIRCLE
(in taupe brown)
Rnd 1 – 5: repeat the pattern for the inner circle.
Do not fasten off. We will join both parts, placing the pale pink circle on the taupe brown circle with the wrong sides together.
Rnd 6: insert the hook under both loops of both circles, sc in all 40 st, ch 1, turn [40]
Rnd 7: slst in all 40 st [40]
Join the last slst to the first slst. Fasten off, leaving a long tail for sewing. Pinch the ears and sew them on top of the head.

TAIL

(in beige)
Rnd 1: start 5 sc in a magic ring [5]
Rnd 2 – 32: sc in all 5 st [5]
Fasten off, leaving a long tail for sewing. Do not stuff.

BLOOMERS

(with off-white fingering weight yarn, using a size B-1 / 2.25 mm crochet hook)
Ch 50 loosely. Make sure your chain isn't twisted. Insert the hook in the first chain stitch and join the foundation chain with a slst. Continue working in a spiral.
Note: I recommend to always check the fitting of the garments. If it doesn't fit, you may want to change the size of the hook, the weight of the yarn or change the number of stitches (add or undo stitches). I know it's more work, but the final result will be better.
Rnd 1 – 2: sc in all 50 st [50]

Rnd 3: (sc in next 4 st, inc in next st) repeat 10 times [60]
Rnd 4: sc in all 60 st [60]
Rnd 5: (sc in next 5 st, inc in next st) repeat 10 times [70]
Rnd 6 – 8: sc in all 70 st [70]
Rnd 9: (sc in next 6 st, inc in next st) repeat 10 times [80]
Rnd 10: ch 6, skip 6 st, sc in next 74 st [80]
Rnd 11 – 18: sc in all 80 st [80]
Do not fasten off.

BLOOMERS LEGS

To make the bloomers legs, divide the work identifying 6 stitches for the central space between the legs, 6 stitches for the back and 34 stitches for each bloomers leg (you may find it useful to use stitch markers). Make sure the hole for the tail in round 10 is centered at the back.
Join the marked stitch for the first bloomers leg on the back side to the marked stitch on the front side, working a single crochet stitch (this sc will be the first stitch of the bloomers leg). Now the stitches of the first bloomers leg are joined in the round. Continue working the first bloomers leg:
Rnd 19 – 20: sc in all 34 st [34]
Rnd 21: (sc in next 15 st, dec) repeat 2 times [32]
Rnd 22 – 23: sc in all 32 st [32]
Rnd 24: (sc in next 2 st, dec) repeat 8 times [24]
Rnd 25: sc in all 24 st [24]
Rnd 26: (4 hdc in next st, slst in next st) repeat 12 times [60]
Fasten off and weave in the yarn ends.

SECOND BLOOMERS LEG

Rejoin the off-white yarn in the seventh unworked stitch at the back of round 18. This is where we start the first stitch of the second bloomers leg. Leave a long starting yarn tail.
Rnd 19: sc in next 34 st. When you reach the 34th stitch of the bloomers leg, sc in first st to join the round [34]
Rnd 20 – 26: repeat the pattern for the first bloomers leg. Fasten off and weave in the yarn ends.
Using a tapestry needle and the starting yarn tail, sew the 6 stitches between the bloomers legs closed.
Put the bloomers on and mark the position of the tail.
Sew the tail to the bottom of the mouse.

DRESS

(start in pastel mint)
Ch 34. Crochet in rows.
Row 1: start in third ch from the hook, hdc in next 32 st, ch 2, turn [32]
Row 2: hdc in next 4 st, ch 6, skip next 6 st, hdc in next 12 st, ch 6, skip next 6 st, hdc in next 4 st, ch 2, turn [32]
Row 3: (hdc in next 3 st, hdc inc in next st) repeat 8 times, ch 2, turn [40]
Row 4: hdc in all 40 st, ch 2, turn [40]
Row 5: (hdc in next 4 st, hdc inc in next st) repeat 8 times [48]
Join the last stitch of row 5 to the first stitch of row 5 with a hdc (this hdc will be the first stitch of the next round). Now the stitches of the dress are joined in the round. Continue working in rounds.
Rnd 6: hdc in all 48 st [48]
Rnd 7: (hdc in next 5 st, hdc inc in next st) repeat 8 times [56]
Rnd 8: hdc in all 56 st [56]
Rnd 9: (hdc in next 6 st, hdc inc in next st) repeat 8 times [64]
Rnd 10: hdc in all 64 st [64]
Note: Work the next round in two colors, pastel mint for the hdc stitches and petrol blue for the 5-dc-bobble. If possible, use the tapestry technique, carrying the petrol blue yarn along on top of the hdc stitches.
Rnd 11: (hdc in next 3 st, 5-dc-bobble in next st) repeat 16 times [64]
Rnd 12: (hdc in next 7 st, hdc inc in next st) repeat 8 times [72]
Rnd 13: sc in all 72 st [72]
Rnd 14: slst in all 72 st [72]
Fasten off and weave in the yarn ends.

Insert your hook in the first stitch on the left side of the neckline, with the right side of the dress facing you. Draw up a loop of pastel mint yarn.
Slip stitch an edge all around the top of the dress: slst in next 32 st across the neckline, slst in next

11 row-ends down the first side, slst in next 10 row-ends up the other side. Ch 5, slst in next st to make the buttonhole. Fasten off and weave in the yarn end.

BUTTON
(in petrol blue)
Rnd 1: start 5 sc in a magic ring [5]
Rnd 2: sc in all 5 st [5]
Fasten off, leaving a long tail for sewing. Using a tapestry needle, weave the yarn tail through the front loop of each remaining stitch and pull tight to close. Sew the button to the back of the dress, opposite the buttonhole.

CAPE

(in graphite gray)
Ch 33. Crochet in rows.
Row 1: start in second ch from the hook, sc in all 32 st, ch 2, turn [32]
Row 2: (hdc in next 7 st, hdc inc in next st) repeat 4 times, ch 2, turn [36]
Row 3: (hdc in next 8 st, hdc inc in next st) repeat 4 times, ch 2, turn [40]
Row 4: (hdc in next 9 st, hdc inc in next st) repeat 4 times, ch 2, turn [44]
Row 5: (hdc in next 10 st, hdc inc in next st) repeat 4 times, ch 2, turn [48]
Row 6: (hdc in next 11 st, hdc inc in next st) repeat 4 times, ch 2, turn [52]
Row 7: (hdc in next 12 st, hdc inc in next st) repeat 4 times, ch 2, turn [56]
Row 8: (hdc in next 13 st, hdc inc in next st) repeat 4 times, ch 2, turn [60]
Row 9: (hdc in next 14 st, hdc inc in next st) repeat 4 times, ch 2, turn [64]
Row 10: hdc in next 4 st, ch 10, skip 10 st, hdc in next st, hdc inc in next st, (hdc in next 15 st, hdc inc in next st) repeat 2 times, hdc in next 2 st, ch 10, skip 10 st, hdc in next 3 st, hdc inc in next st, ch 2, turn [68]
Row 11: hdc in all 68 st, ch 2, turn [68]
Row 12: (hdc in next 16 st, hdc inc in next st) repeat 4 times, ch 2, turn [72]
Row 13: hdc in all 72 st [72]
Without turning, ch 1, sc in the row-ends up the first side (about 20 sc), ch 25 to make the cape strap, start in second ch from the hook, slst in next 24 ch, sc in the stitch where the foundation chain starts, continue on the neckline: (4 hdc in next st, skip 1 st, slst in next st, skip 1 st) repeat 8 times, 4 hdc in next st. Ch 25 to make the other cape strap, start in second ch from the hook, slst in next 24 ch, sc in the stitch where the foundation chain starts, sc down the row-ends on the other side (about 20 sc), slst in all 72 st across row 13 of the cape. Fasten off and weave in the yarn ends.

Horacio Polar Bear

Horacio's parents are musicians so ever since he was a little cub, he has been touring the world. At first, he didn't like being away from his polar home. Horacio missed his favorite foods and his dear friends. With time, Horacio made the search for delicious food and coffee part of his traveling routine, getting to know the markets and the places where the locals eat. And he discovered something wonderful: everyone is happy and makes new friends when there's food around. Lots of friendships grew from his encounters. Since he can't live without his morning coffee, he now dedicates his life to this routine: he studies the varieties, crops and ways of preparing coffee, with an eye for sustainability, the environment and social rights. His job now is the perfect excuse to continue traveling, meet new people and visit old acquaintances.

GALLERY: Scan or visit *www.amigurumi.com/4104* to share pictures and find inspiration.

SKILL LEVEL *

Size:
12.5 inches / 31 cm tall when made with the indicated yarn (ears included)

Materials:
– Worsted weight yarn in
  · off-white
  · navy blue
  · white
  · pastel pink (leftover)
  · black (leftover)
  · yellow
– Size C-2 / 2.75 mm crochet hook
– Black safety eyes (10 mm)
– Tapestry needle
– Fiberfill

Skills needed: magic ring *(page 32)*, changing color at the beginning of a round *(page 35)*, joining parts *(page 39)*, dividing the body in 2 parts *(page 47)*, griddle stitch *(explained in pattern)*, embroidery *(page 38)*

Note: The head and body are worked in one piece.

SNOUT

(in off-white)
Rnd 1: start 8 sc in a magic ring [8]
Rnd 2: inc in all 8 st [16]
Rnd 3 – 7: sc in all 16 st [16]
Fasten off, leaving a long tail for sewing. Embroider the nose and mouth with black yarn.

HEAD AND BODY

(start in off-white)
Rnd 1: start 6 sc in a magic ring [6]
Rnd 2: inc in all 6 st [12]
Rnd 3: (sc in next st, inc in next st) repeat 6 times [18]
Rnd 4: (sc in next 2 st, inc in next st) repeat 6 times [24]
Rnd 5: (sc in next 3 st, inc in next st) repeat 6 times [30]
Rnd 6: (sc in next 4 st, inc in next st) repeat 6 times [36]
Rnd 7: (sc in next 5 st, inc in next st) repeat 6 times [42]
Rnd 8: (sc in next 6 st, inc in next st) repeat 6 times [48]
Rnd 9: (sc in next 7 st, inc in next st) repeat 6 times [54]
Rnd 10 – 23: sc in all 54 st [54]
Sew the snout between rounds 13 and 18. Stuff the snout with fiberfill before closing the seam. Insert the safety eyes between rounds 14 and 15, about 3 stitches away from the snout. Embroider the cheeks with pastel pink yarn.
Rnd 24: (sc in next 8 st, inc in next st) repeat 6 times [60]
Continue working in a stripe pattern, alternating 1 round in navy blue and 2 rounds in white yarn.
Rnd 25 – 27: sc in all 60 st [60]
Rnd 28: (sc in next 9 st, inc in next st) repeat 6 times [66]
Rnd 29 – 33: sc in all 66 st [66]
Rnd 34: (sc in next 10 st, inc in next st) repeat 6 times [72]
Rnd 35 – 42: sc in all 72 st [72]
Change to pastel pink yarn.
Rnd 43: sc in all 72 st [72]
Change to off-white yarn.
Rnd 44: BLO (sc in next 11 st, inc in next st) repeat 6 times [78]
Rnd 45 – 51: sc in all 78 st [78]
Rnd 52: (sc in next 11 st, dec) repeat 6 times [72]
Rnd 53 – 55: sc in all 72 st [72]
Rnd 56: (sc in next 10 st, dec) repeat 6 times [66]

Rnd 57 – 59: sc in all 66 st [66]
Rnd 60: (sc in next 9 st, dec) repeat 6 times [60]
Rnd 61 – 62: sc in all 60 st [60]
Rnd 63: (sc in next 8 st, dec) repeat 6 times [54]
Rnd 64: sc in all 54 st [54]
Do not fasten off.

LEGS

To make the legs, divide the work identifying 6 stitches for the front central space between the legs, 6 stitches for the back and 21 stitches for each leg (you may find it useful to use stitch markers). If the legs don't line up nicely with the head, crochet a few more sc on the body or undo them. Join the marked stitch for the first leg on the back side to the marked stitch on the front side, working a single crochet stitch (this sc will be the first stitch of the leg). Now the stitches of the first leg are joined in the round. Continue working the first leg:
Rnd 65 – 72: sc in all 21 st [21]
Stuff the body and leg firmly.
Rnd 73: (sc in next st, dec) repeat 7 times [14]
Rnd 74: dec 7 times [7]
Fasten off, leaving a long tail. Using a tapestry needle, weave the yarn tail through the front loop of each remaining stitch and pull tight to close. Weave in the yarn end. Stuff the body and the first leg.

SECOND LEG
Rejoin the off-white yarn in the seventh un-worked stitch at the back of round 64. This is where we start the first stitch of the second leg. Leave a long starting yarn tail.
Rnd 65: sc in next 21 st. When you reach the 21st stitch of the leg, sc in first st to join the round [21]
Rnd 66 – 74: repeat the pattern for the first leg. Add more stuffing to the body if needed. Using a tapestry needle and the starting yarn tail, sew the 6 stitches between the legs closed.

ARMS

(make 2, start in off-white)
Rnd 1: start 5 sc in a magic ring [5]
Rnd 2: inc in all 5 st [10]
Rnd 3: (sc in next st, inc in next st) repeat 5 times [15]
Rnd 4 – 5: sc in all 15 st [15]
Rnd 6: sc in next st, 5-dc-bobble in next st, sc in next 13 st [15]
Rnd 7 – 18: sc in all 15 st [15]
Change to navy blue yarn and continue working in a stripe pattern, alternating 1 round in navy blue and 2 rounds in white yarn.
Rnd 19 – 23: sc in all 15 st [15]
Rnd 24: (sc in next st, dec) repeat 5 times [10]
Fasten off, leaving a long tail for sewing. Stuff with fiberfill. Sew the arms to both sides between rounds 26 and 27.

EARS

(make 2, in off-white)
Rnd 1: start 5 sc in a magic ring [5]
Rnd 2: inc in all 5 st [10]
Rnd 3 – 5: sc in all 10 st [10]
Fasten off, leaving a long tail for sewing. The ears do not need to be stuffed. Flatten the ears before sewing. Sew them to the top of the head, between rounds 3 and 8.

TAIL

(in off-white)
Rnd 1: start 5 sc in a magic ring [5]
Rnd 2 – 4: sc in all 5 st [5]
Fasten off, leaving a long tail for sewing. Do not stuff. Sew the tail to the back, centered between rounds 50 and 51.

TROUSERS

(start in yellow)

Ch 72. Make sure your stitches aren't too tight and that your chain isn't twisted. Insert the hook in the first chain stitch and join the foundation chain with a slst. Continue working in a spiral.

Note: The trousers are made using the griddle stitch, by alternating 1 sc and 1 dc. As you start the next round, remember that you always work a dc into a sc of the previous round and vice versa.

Rnd 1: (sc in next st, dc in next st) repeat this until the end of the round [72]
Change to white yarn.
Rnd 2: (dc in next st, sc in next st) repeat this until the end of the round [72]
Change to yellow yarn.
Rnd 3 – 17: repeat rounds 1 and 2 (including the color changes).
Do not fasten off.

TROUSER LEGS

To make the trouser legs, divide the work identifying 6 stitches for the front central space between the legs, 6 stitches for the back and 30 stitches for each trouser leg (you may find it useful to use stitch markers). Join the first marked stitch for the trouser leg on the back side to the marked stitch on the front side, working a single crochet stitch (this sc will be the first stitch of the trouser leg). Now the stitches of the first trouser leg are joined in the round. Continue working the first trouser leg:
Note: Depending on where you divide the trousers, you'll have to start round 18 with a sc or a dc stitch, it makes no difference for the end result.
Rnd 18: work the griddle stitch in next 30 st [30]
Change to yellow yarn.
Rnd 19: (sc in next 4 st, dec) repeat 5 times [25]
Rnd 20: sc in all 25 st [25]
Rnd 21: slst in all 25 st [25]
Fasten off and weave in the yarn ends.

SECOND TROUSER LEG

Rejoin the white yarn in the seventh unworked stitch at the back of round 17. This is where we start the first stitch of the second trouser leg. Leave a long starting yarn tail.

Rnd 18 – 21: repeat the pattern for the first trouser leg.
Fasten off and weave in the yarn ends. Using a tapestry needle and the starting yarn tail, sew the 6 stitches between the trouser legs closed.

WAISTBAND
(in pastel pink)
Join pastel pink yarn in the first stitch of round 1 of the trousers.
Rnd 1 – 2: sc in all 72 st [72]
Rnd 3: BLO slst in all 72 st [72]
Fasten off and weave in the yarn ends.

SHOULDER STRAPS
(make 2, start in yellow)
Ch 49. Crochet in rows.
Row 1: start in second ch from the hook, slst in all 48 st, ch 1, turn [48]
Change to white yarn.
Row 2 – 3: BLO slst in all 48 st, ch 1, turn [48]
Change to yellow yarn.
Row 4: BLO slst in all 48 st, ch 1, turn [48]
Row 5: BLO slst in all 48 st [48]
Fasten off, leaving a long tail for sewing. Sew one end of the shoulder strap to the front of the trousers, on the inside of the pastel pink waistband. Sew the other end to the back of the trousers, at about 15 stitches from the first end.

Ron Red Panda

Ron is kind of a chatterbox. He jabbers about anything. Really, anything that comes to his mind. He's curious, so he reads a lot. Like: all day long. And again: everything. Especially silly facts, things that hardly anyone cares to read about. And he's great at remembering all that stuff, including the most capricious details. He's also great at repairing things. Perhaps for the same reason he can remember every minor detail, he can also repair all things that others gave up on. Like that faucet that keeps dripping, or the irritating noise the closet door makes, specifically at 6 in the morning when you are trying not to wake the whole family. Yes, you may say Ron is the best Handy Andy Red Panda, and the most chattery as well.

GALLERY: Scan or visit *www.amigurumi.com/4105* to share pictures and find inspiration.

SKILL LEVEL **

Size:
10.5 inches / 27 cm tall when made with the indicated yarn (ears included)

Materials:
– Worsted weight yarn in
· burnt orange
· off-white
· brick red
· black (leftover)
· pastel pink
· cream
· graphite gray
· yellow (leftover)
– Size C-2 / 2.75 mm crochet hook
– Size E-4 / 3.5 mm crochet hook
– Black safety eyes (10 mm)
– Tapestry needle
– Fiberfill

Skills needed: magic ring *(page 32)*, working around a foundation chain *(page 34)*, changing color at the beginning of a round *(page 35)*, changing color mid-round *(page 35)*, half double slip stitch *(page 26)*, joining parts *(page 39)*, dividing the body in two parts *(page 47)*, embroidery *(page 38)*

Note: The head and body are worked in one piece.

Note: Use a size C-2 / 2.75 mm crochet hook, unless otherwise noted.

CHEEKS

(make 2, in pastel pink)
Rnd 1: start 6 sc in a magic ring [6] Slst in next st. Fasten off, leaving a long tail for sewing.

SNOUT

(in off-white)
Ch 6. Stitches are worked around both sides of the foundation chain.
Rnd 1: start in second ch from the hook, sc in next 4 st, 3 sc in last st. Continue on the other side of the foundation chain, sc in next 3 st, inc in last st [12]
Rnd 2: inc in next st, sc in next 3 st, inc in next 3 st, sc in next 3 st, inc in next 2 st [18]
Rnd 3 – 4: sc in all 18 st [18]

Fasten off, leaving a long tail for sewing. Embroider the mouth and nose with black yarn.

HEAD AND BODY

(start in burnt orange)
Rnd 1: start 6 sc in a magic ring [6]
Rnd 2: inc in all 6 st [12]
Rnd 3: (sc in next st, inc in next st) repeat 6 times [18]
Rnd 4: (sc in next st, inc in next st) repeat 9 times [27]
Rnd 5: (sc in next 2 st, inc in next st) repeat 9 times [36]
Rnd 6: (sc in next 3 st, inc in next st) repeat 9 times [45]
Rnd 7: (sc in next 4 st, inc in next st) repeat 9 times [54]
Rnd 8: (sc in next 8 st, inc in next st) repeat 6 times [60]
Rnd 9 – 11: sc in all 60 st [60]
Continue working with alternating yarns (burnt orange and off-white). The color you work with is indicated before each part.
Rnd 12: *(burnt orange)* (sc in next 9 st, inc in next st) repeat 2 times, sc in next 2 st, *(off-white)* sc in next 4 st, *(burnt orange)* sc in next 3 st, inc in next st, sc in next 5 st, *(off-white)* sc in next 4 st, *(burnt orange)* inc in next st, (sc in next 9 st, inc in next st) repeat 2 times [66]
Rnd 13: *(burnt orange)* sc in next 22 st, *(off-white)*

sc in next 7 st, *(burnt orange)* sc in next 8 st, *(off-white)* sc in next 7 st, *(burnt orange)* sc in next 22 st [66]

Rnd 14: *(burnt orange)* sc in next 21 st, *(off-white)* sc in next 7 st, *(burnt orange)* sc in next 10 st, *(off-white)* sc in next 7 st, *(burnt orange)* sc in next 21 st [66]

Rnd 15 – 16: *(burnt orange)* sc in next 20 st, *(off-white)* sc in next 3 st, *(burnt orange)* sc in next 20 st, *(off-white)* sc in next 3 st, *(burnt orange)* sc in next 20 st [66]

Rnd 17: *(burnt orange)* sc in next 19 st, *(off-white)* sc in next 4 st, *(burnt orange)* sc in next 20 st, *(off-white)* sc in next 4 st, *(burnt orange)* sc in next 19 st [66]

Rnd 18: *(burnt orange)* sc in next 18 st, *(off-white)* sc in next 4 st, *(burnt orange)* sc in next 22 st, *(off-white)* sc in next 4 st, *(burnt orange)* sc in next 18 st [66]

Rnd 19 – 20: *(burnt orange)* sc in next 17 st, *(off-white)* sc in next 5 st, *(burnt orange)* sc in next 22 st, *(off-white)* sc in next 5 st, *(burnt orange)* sc in next 17 st [66]

Rnd 21: *(burnt orange)* sc in next 17 st, *(off-white)* sc in next 6 st, *(burnt orange)* sc in next 20 st, *(off-white)* sc in next 6 st, *(burnt orange)* sc in next 17 st [66]

Rnd 22: *(burnt orange)* sc in next 18 st, *(off-white)* sc in next 6 st, *(burnt orange)* sc in next 18 st, *(off-white)* sc in next 6 st, *(burnt orange)* sc in next 18 st [66]

Rnd 23: *(burnt orange)* sc in next 9 st, dec, sc in next 8 st, *(off-white)* sc in next st, dec, sc in next 3 st, *(burnt orange)* sc in next 6 st, dec, sc in next 8 st, *(off-white)* sc in next st, dec, sc in next 3 st, *(burnt orange)* sc in next 6 st, dec, sc in next 9 st, dec [60]

Rnd 24: *(burnt orange)* (sc in next 3 st, dec) repeat 3 times, sc in next 3 st, *(off-white)* dec, sc in next 3 st, dec, *(burnt orange)* (sc in next 3 st, dec) repeat 2 times, sc in next 2 st, *(off-white)* sc in next st, dec, sc in next 3 st, *(burnt orange)* dec, (sc in next 3 st, dec) repeat 3 times [48]
Continue in burnt orange yarn.

Rnd 25: (sc in next 2 st, dec) repeat 12 times [36]
Sew the snout between rounds 15 and 20. Stuff

the snout with fiberfill before closing the seam. Insert the safety eyes between rounds 16 and 17, about 3 stitches away from the snout. Sew the cheeks below the safety eyes.

Rnd 26: (sc in next 4 st, dec) repeat 6 times [30]

Rnd 27: (sc in next 3 st, dec) repeat 6 times [24]

Rnd 28: sc in all 24 st [24]
Stuff the head firmly.

Rnd 29: (sc in next 2 st, inc in next st) repeat 8 times [32]

Rnd 30: sc in all 32 st [32]

Rnd 31: (sc in next 3 st, inc in next st) repeat 8 times [40]

Rnd 32 – 34: sc in all 40 st [40]

Rnd 35: (sc in next 9 st, inc in next st) repeat 4 times [44]

Rnd 36 – 39: sc in all 44 st [44]

Rnd 40: (sc in next 10 st, inc in next st) repeat 4 times [48]

Rnd 41 – 49: sc in all 48 st [48]

Rnd 50: (sc in next 6 st, dec) repeat 6 times [42]

Rnd 51 – 53: sc in all 42 st [42]
Change to brick red yarn.

Rnd 54: sc in all 42 st [42]
Do not fasten off.

LEGS

To make the legs, divide the work identifying 3 stitches for the front central space between the legs, 3 stitches for the back and 18 stitches for each leg (you may find it useful to use stitch markers). If the legs don't line up nicely with the head, crochet a few more sc on the body or undo them. Join the first marked stitch for the leg on the back side to the marked stitch on the front side, working a single crochet stitch (this sc will be the first stitch of the leg). Now the stitches of the first leg are joined in the round. Continue working the first leg:

Rnd 55 – 62: sc in all 18 st [18]
Stuff the body and leg firmly.

Rnd 63: (sc in next st, dec) repeat 6 times [12]

Rnd 64: dec 6 times [6]
Fasten off, leaving a long tail. Using a tapestry needle, weave the yarn tail through the front loop of each remaining stitch and pull tight to close. Weave in the yarn end.

SECOND LEG
Rejoin the brick red yarn to the fourth unworked stitch at the back of round 54. This is where we start the first stitch of the second leg. Leave a long starting yarn tail.

Rnd 55: sc in next 18 st. When you reach the 18th st of the leg, sc in first st to join the round [18]
Rnd 56 – 64: repeat the pattern for the first leg.
Stuff the second leg and add more stuffing to the body if needed. Using a tapestry needle and the starting yarn tail, sew the 3 stitches between the legs closed.

ARMS

(make 2, start in brick red)
Rnd 1: start 6 sc in a magic ring [6]
Rnd 2: inc in all 6 st [12]
Rnd 3 – 4: sc in all 12 st [12]
Rnd 5: sc in next st, 5-dc-bobble in next st, sc in next 10 st [12]
Rnd 6: sc in all 12 st [12]
Change to burnt orange yarn.
Rnd 7 – 17: sc in all 12 st [12]
Rnd 18: (sc in next 4 st, dec) repeat 2 times [10]
Fasten off, leaving a long tail for sewing. Stuff with fiberfill. Sew the arms to both sides between rounds 30 and 31.

EARS

(make 2, start in off-white)
Rnd 1: start 6 sc in a magic ring [6]
Continue working with alternating yarns (off-white and brick red). The color you work with is indicated before each part.
Rnd 2: *(off-white)* inc in next 3 st, *(brick red)* inc in next 3 st [12]
Rnd 3: *(off-white)* sc in next 6 st, *(brick red)* sc in next 6 st [12]
Rnd 4: *(off-white)* (sc in next st, inc in next st) repeat 3 times, *(brick red)* (sc in next st, inc in next st) repeat 3 times [18]
Rnd 5: *(off-white)* sc in next 9 st, *(brick red)* sc in next 9 st [18]
Rnd 6: *(off-white)* (sc in next 2 st, inc in next st) repeat 3 times, *(brick red)* (sc in next 2 st, inc in next st) repeat 3 times [24]
Rnd 7 – 8: *(off-white)* sc in next 12 st, *(brick red)* sc in next 12 st [24]
Fasten off, leaving a long tail for sewing. The ears do not need to be stuffed. Embroider burnt orange stripes on the white part of the ear. Flatten the ears before sewing them to the head.

TAIL

(start in brick red)
Rnd 1: start 6 sc in a magic ring [6]
Rnd 2: inc in all 6 st [12]
Rnd 3: (sc in next st, inc in next st) repeat 6 times [18]
Rnd 4: (sc in next 2 st, inc in next st) repeat 6 times [24]
Rnd 5: (sc in next 3 st, inc in next st) repeat 6 times [30]
Rnd 6 – 7: sc in all 30 st [30]
Change to burnt orange yarn and continue working in a stripe pattern, alternating 3 rounds in burnt orange and 3 rounds in brick red yarn. Stuff the tail and continue stuffing as you go.
Rnd 8 – 28: sc in all 30 st [30]
Rnd 29: (sc in next 8 st, dec) repeat 3 times [27]
Rnd 30 – 34: sc in all 27 st [27]
Rnd 35: (sc in next 7 st, dec) repeat 3 times [24]
Rnd 36 – 37: sc in all 24 st [24]
Rnd 38: (sc in next 6 st, dec) repeat 3 times [21]
Rnd 39 – 40: sc in all 21 st [21]
Fasten off, leaving a long tail for sewing. Stuff with fiberfill, but stuff less at the top. Sew the tail to the back, centered over rounds 46 to 49.

TROUSERS

(start in cream)
Ch 52. Make sure your chain isn't twisted. Insert the hook in the first chain stitch and join the foundation chain with a slst. Continue working in a spiral.
Rnd 1: sc in all 52 st [52]
Change to graphite gray yarn.
Rnd 2: (sc in all 12 st, inc in next st) repeat 4 times [56]
Continue working in a stripe pattern, alternating 2 rounds in cream and 1 round in graphite gray yarn.

single crochet stitch (this sc will be the first stitch of the trouser leg). Now the stitches of the first trouser leg are joined in the round. Continue working the first trouser leg:

Rnd 15 – 17: sc in all 24 st [24]
Continue in graphite gray.
Rnd 18: BLO slst in all 24 st [24]
Fasten off and weave in the yarn ends.

SECOND TROUSER LEG

Rejoin the cream yarn in the fifth unworked stitch at the back of round 14. This is where we start the first stitch of the second trouser leg. Leave a long starting yarn tail.

Rnd 15: sc in next 24 st. When you reach the 24th st on the trouser leg, sc in first st to join the round [24]
Rnd 16 – 18: repeat the pattern for the first trouser leg.

Using a tapestry needle and the starting yarn tail, sew the 4 stitches between the trouser legs closed.

WAISTBAND
(in yellow)

Join yellow yarn in the first stitch of round 1.
Rnd 1 – 2: sc in all 52 st [52]
Rnd 3: slst in all 52 st [52]
Fasten off and weave in the yarn ends.

SCARF

(using a 3.5 mm crochet hook, in brick red)
Ch 108. Crochet in rows.
Row 1: start in third ch from the hook, hdslst in next 106 st, ch 1, turn [106]
Row 2 – 8: BLO hdslst in all 106 st, ch 1, turn [106]
Fasten off and weave in the yarn ends.

Make two 2" / 5 cm pompons in pastel pink yarn. Sew one pompon to each end of the scarf.

Rnd 3 – 7: sc in all 56 st [56]
Rnd 8: sc in next st, ch 10, skip next 10 st, sc in next 45 st [56]
Rnd 9 – 14: sc in all 56 st [56]
Do not fasten off.

TROUSER LEGS

To make the trouser legs, divide the work identifying 4 stitches for the central space between the legs, 4 stitches for the back and 24 stitches for each trouser leg (you may find it useful to use stitch markers). Make sure the hole for the tail in round 8 is centered at the back. Join the first marked stitch for the trouser leg on the back side to the marked stitch on the front side, working a

Angus Squirrel

Proud Scotsman and breakfast fan, Angus believes that the "elevenses" (the pastries, fruits, toast and tea he has as a little snack between breakfast and lunch) is essential to maintain a good mood during the day. He's a follower of the hobbit philosophy of life: relax, enjoy things as they come and do so with a lot of food involved. Angus has set up his own grocery store, the perfect enterprise if you want to have the best and freshest produce at hand. He is so good at picking fresh products and has the peculiarity to try everything he sells, his grocery store is the most amazing and colorful store in town.

 GALLERY: Scan or visit *www.amigurumi.com/4106* to share pictures and find inspiration.

SKILL LEVEL *

Size:
10 inches / 25 cm tall when made with the indicated yarn (ears included)

Materials:
– Worsted weight yarn in
  · mustard yellow
  · off-white
  · white
  · navy blue
  · brown (leftover)
  · black (leftover)
– Size C-2 / 2.75 mm crochet hook
– Black safety eyes (8 mm)
– Tapestry needle
– Fiberfill

Skills needed: magic ring (page 32), changing color at the beginning of a round (page 35), changing color mid-round (page 35), dividing the body in two parts (page 47), joining parts (page 39), embroidery (page 38),

Note: The head and body are worked in one piece.

SNOUT

(start in off-white yarn)
Rnd 1: start 6 sc in a magic ring [6]
Continue working with alternating yarns (off-white and mustard yellow). The color you work with is indicated before each part.
Rnd 2: *(off-white)* inc in next 3 st, *(mustard yellow)* inc in next 2 st, *(off-white)* inc in next st [12]
Rnd 3: *(off-white)* (sc in next st, inc in next st) repeat 3 times, *(mustard yellow)* (sc in next st, inc in next st) repeat 2 times, *(off-white)* sc in next st, inc in next st [18]
Rnd 4: *(off-white)* sc in next 9 st, *(mustard yellow)* sc in next 6 st, *(off-white)* sc in next 3 st [18]
Sc in next 2 st (to create space to embroider the mouth) and fasten off, leaving a long tail for sewing. Embroider the nose and mouth with black yarn.

HEAD AND BODY

(start in mustard yellow)
Rnd 1: start 6 sc in a magic ring [6]
Rnd 2: inc in all 6 st [12]
Rnd 3: (sc in next st, inc in next st) repeat 6 times [18]
Rnd 4: (sc in next 2 st, inc in next st) repeat 6 times [24]
Rnd 5: (sc in next 3 st, inc in next st) repeat 6 times [30]
Rnd 6: (sc in next 4 st, inc in next st) repeat 6 times [36]
Rnd 7: (sc in next 5 st, inc in next st) repeat 6 times [42]
Rnd 8: (sc in next 6 st, inc in next st) repeat 6 times [48]
Rnd 9 – 14: sc in all 48 st [48]
Change to off-white yarn.
Rnd 15: (sc in next 3 st, inc in next st) repeat 12 times [60]
Rnd 16: (sc in next 4 st, inc in next st) repeat 12 times [72]
Rnd 17 – 18: sc in all 72 st [72]
Rnd 19: (sc in next 2 st, dec) repeat 18 times [54]
Rnd 20: (sc in next 7 st, dec) repeat 6 times [48]

Rnd 21: (sc in next 2 st, dec) repeat 12 times [36]

Sew the snout between rounds 13 and 18. The snout must be placed on the opposite side of the start of the round. Stuff the snout with fiberfill before closing the seam. Insert the safety eyes between rounds 14 and 15, about 2 stitches away from the snout. Embroider 2 lines next to each eye and short lines on the forehead with brown yarn.

Rnd 22: (sc in next 4 st, dec) repeat 6 times [30]

Rnd 23: (sc in next st, dec) repeat 10 times [20]

Rnd 24: sc in all 20 st [20]

Stuff the head firmly. Continue in a stripe pattern, changing color every round, alternating navy blue and white yarn.

Rnd 25: (sc in next st, inc in next st) repeat 10 times [30]

Rnd 26: sc in all 30 st [30]

Rnd 27: (sc in next 4 st, inc in next st) repeat 6 times [36]

Rnd 28 – 30: sc in all 36 st [36]

Rnd 31: (sc in next 8 st, inc in next st) repeat 4 times [40]

Rnd 32 – 36: sc in all 40 st [40]

Change to mustard yellow yarn.

Rnd 37: BLO (sc in next 9 st, inc in next st) repeat 4 times [44]

Rnd 38 – 50: sc in all 44 st [44]

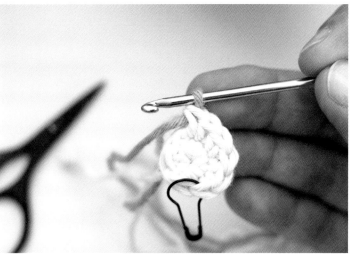

Rnd 51: (sc in next 9 st, dec) repeat 4 times [40]
Rnd 52 – 54: sc in all 40 st [40]
Do not fasten off.

LEGS

To make the legs, divide the work identifying 4 stitches for the front central space between the legs, 4 stitches for the back and 16 stitches for each leg (you may find it useful to use stitch markers). If the legs don't line up nicely with the head, crochet a few more sc on the body or undo them. Join the first marked stitch for the leg on the back side to the marked stitch on the front side, working a single crochet stitch (this sc will be the first stitch of the leg). Now the stitches of the first leg are joined in the round. Continue working the first leg:
Rnd 55 – 59: sc in all 16 st [16]
Stuff the body and leg firmly.
Rnd 60: (sc in next 2 st, dec) repeat 4 times [12]
Rnd 61: dec 6 times [6]
Fasten off, leaving a long tail. Using a tapestry needle, weave the yarn tail through the front loop of each remaining stitch and pull tight to close. Weave in the yarn end.

SECOND LEG
Rejoin the mustard yellow yarn in the fifth unworked stitch at the back of round 54. This is where we start the first stitch of the second leg. Leave a long starting yarn tail.
Rnd 55: sc in next 16 st. When you reach the 16th stitch of the leg, sc in first st to join the round [16]
Rnd 56 – 61: repeat the pattern for the first leg.
Stuff the second leg and add more stuffing to the body if needed. Using a tapestry needle and the starting yarn tail, sew the 4 stitches between the legs closed.

ARMS

(make 2, start in mustard yellow)
Rnd 1: start 5 sc in a magic ring [5]
Rnd 2: inc in all 5 st [10]
Rnd 3 – 9: sc in all 10 st [10]
Continue in a stripe pattern, changing color every round, alternating white and navy blue yarn.
Rnd 10 – 17: sc in all 10 st [10]
Rnd 18: (sc in next 3 st, dec) repeat 2 times [8]
Fasten off, leaving a long tail for sewing. Stuff with fiberfill. Sew the arms to both sides between rounds 26 and 27.

EARS

(in mustard yellow)
Rnd 1: start 6 sc in a magic ring [6]
Rnd 2: inc in all 6 st [12]
Rnd 3 – 5: sc in all 12 st [12]
Fasten off, leaving a long tail for sewing. The ears do not need to be stuffed. Embroider off-white stripes on the inside of the ear. Flatten before sewing them to the head.

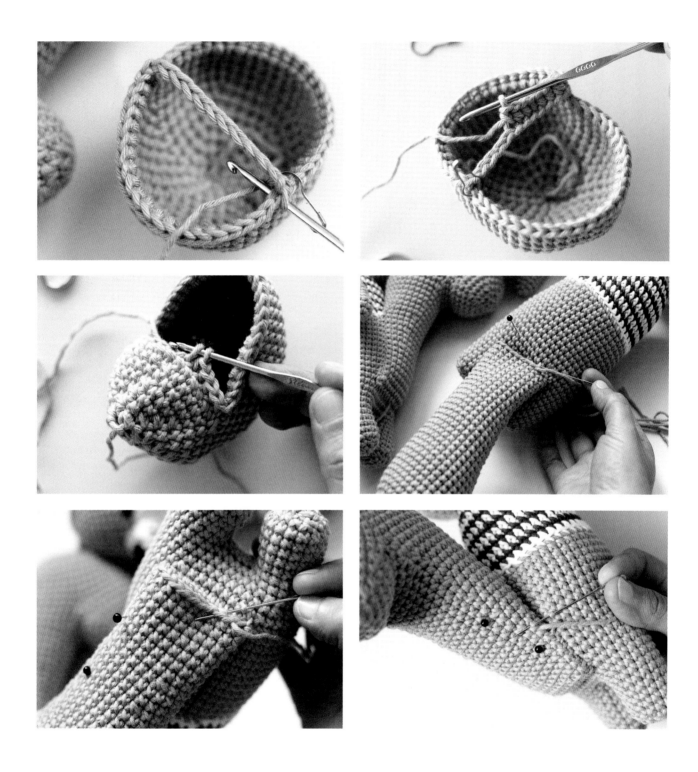

TAIL

(in mustard yellow)
The tail is made by starting at the top, which is then split into two parts, the tip and the base.
Rnd 1: start 6 sc in a magic ring [6]
Rnd 2: inc in all 6 st [12]
Rnd 3: (sc in next st, inc in next st) repeat 6 times [18]
Rnd 4: (sc in next 2 st, inc in next st) repeat 6 times [24]
Rnd 5: (sc in next 3 st, inc in next st) repeat 6 times [30]
Rnd 6: (sc in next 4 st, inc in next st) repeat 6 times [36]
Rnd 7: (sc in next 5 st, inc in next st) repeat 6 times [42]
Rnd 8: (sc in next 6 st, inc in next st) repeat 6 times [48]
Rnd 9 – 12: sc in all 48 st [48]
Do not fasten off, we continue with the tip of the tail.

TIP OF THE TAIL

Ch 12. Skip 26 st and join to the 27th stitch of round 12 with a sc. The tip will be formed with 22 stitches of the top part and the ch-12 foundation chain. Continue working the tip of the tail:
Rnd 1: sc in all 34 st (22 on the top part and 12 on the chain) [34]
Rnd 2: (dec, sc in next 8 st) repeat 2 times, (dec, sc in next 5 st) repeat 2 times [30]
Rnd 3: sc in all 30 st [30]

Rnd 4: (sc in next 3 st, dec) repeat 6 times [24]
Rnd 5: (sc in next 2 st, dec) repeat 6 times [18]
Rnd 6: (sc in next st, dec) repeat 6 times [12]
Rnd 7: dec 6 times [6]
Fasten off, leaving a long tail. Using a tapestry needle, weave the yarn tail through the front loop of each remaining stitch and pull tight to close. Weave in the yarn end.

BASE OF THE TAIL

Rejoin the mustard yellow yarn to the first stitch to the left of the tip of the tail, on round 12.
Rnd 13: sc in next 26 st, FLO sc in next 12 ch, sc in first st to join the round [38]
Rnd 14: sc in next 26 st, dec, sc in next 8 st, dec [36]
Rnd 15: sc in next 26 st, dec, sc in next 6 st, dec [34]
Rnd 16: dec, sc in next 24 st, dec, sc in next 6 st [32]
Rnd 17: dec, sc in next 22 st, dec, sc in next 6 st [30]
Rnd 18 – 19: sc in all 30 st [30]
Rnd 20: dec, sc in next 20 st, dec, sc in next 6 st [28]
Rnd 21 – 22: sc in all 28 st [28]
Stuff the tip and the top part of the tail.
Rnd 23: dec, sc in next 18 st, dec, sc in next 6 st [26]
Rnd 24 – 25: sc in all 26 st [26]
Rnd 26: dec, sc in next 16 st, dec, sc in next 6 st [24]
Rnd 27 – 28: sc in all 24 st [24]
Rnd 29: dec, sc in next 14 st, dec, sc in next 6 st [22]
Rnd 30 – 36: sc in all 22 st [22]
Fasten off, leaving a (very) long tail for sewing. Stuff the base part of the tail, but do not overstuff when you reach the open edge. Flatten the open edge. Sew the tail to the back, centered over rounds 35 to 51. First sew the inner edge of the tail to round 50 (sew from the right to the left side). Then sew the outer edge of the tail to round 51 (left to right). Sew up the side, attaching the side of the tail to round 51 up to round 35. Sew from right to left on round 35. Sew down the side, attaching the side of the tail to round 35, down to round 51. Weave in the yarn ends.

Humboldt Penguin

Humboldt was named after one of the greatest explorers and natural geographers in modern history, Sir Friedrich Wilhelm Heinrich Alexander von Humboldt. Quite a name. So, to honor such an important and long name, our dear Humboldt Penguin is determined to become a geographer, naturalist and explorer of all the oceans on the planet. His goal is to become Sir von Humboldt II, travelling and exploring the unknown. His friends suspect his actual desire is to try all varieties of fish that he finds on his way. Whatever his motivation, no one doubts his enthusiasm, as he spends most of his days perfecting his swimming techniques and drawing naturalistic illustrations. He has gotten quite good at drawing, mostly fish.

 GALLERY: Scan or visit www.amigurumi.com/4107 to share pictures and find inspiration.

Size:
9 inches / 23 cm tall when made with the indicated yarn

Materials:
– Worsted weight yarn in
  · petrol blue
  · off-white
  · greenish gray
  · red
  · yellow
  · pastel pink (leftover)
– Size C-2 / 2.75 mm crochet hook
– Size E-4 / 3.5 mm crochet hook
– Oval black safety eyes (12 mm)
– Tapestry needle
– Fiberfill

Skills needed: magic ring (page 32), working around a foundation chain (page 34), changing color mid-round (page 35), changing color at the beginning of a round (page 35), dividing the body in 2 parts (page 47), embroidery (page 38), joining parts (page 39), working in the back ridge of a chain (page 20), working half double slip stitch (page 26)

Note: Use a size C-2 / 2.75 mm crochet hook, unless otherwise noted.

Note: The head and body are worked in one piece.

BEAK

(in yellow)
Rnd 1: start 8 sc in a magic ring [8]
Rnd 2: sc in all 8 st [8]
Slst in next st. Fasten off, leaving a long tail for sewing. Do not stuff.

CHEEKS

(make 2, in pastel pink)
Rnd 1: start 8 sc in a magic ring [8]
Slst in next st. Fasten off, leaving a long tail for sewing.

HEAD AND BODY

(start in petrol blue)
Rnd 1: start 6 sc in a magic ring [6]
Rnd 2: inc in all 6 st [12]
Rnd 3: (sc in next st, inc in next st) repeat 6 times [18]
Rnd 4: (sc in next 2 st, inc in next st) repeat 6 times [24]
Rnd 5: (sc in next 3 st, inc in next st) repeat 6 times [30]
Rnd 6: (sc in next 4 st, inc in next st) repeat 6 times [36]
Rnd 7: (sc in next 5 st, inc in next st) repeat 6 times [42]
Rnd 8: (sc in next 6 st, inc in next st) repeat 6 times [48]
Rnd 9: sc in all 48 st [48]
Continue working with alternating yarns (petrol blue and off-white). The color you work with is indicated before each part.
Rnd 10: *(petrol blue)* sc in next 16 st, *(off-white)* sc in next 4 st, *(petrol blue)* sc in next 8 st, *(off-white)* sc in next 4 st, *(petrol blue)* sc in next 16 st [48]
Rnd 11: *(petrol blue)* sc in next 15 st, *(off-white)* sc in next 6 st, *(petrol blue)* sc in next 6 st, *(off-white)* sc in next 6 st, *(petrol blue)* sc in next 15 st [48]
Rnd 12 – 14: *(petrol blue)* sc in next 14 st, *(off-white)* sc in next 8 st, *(petrol blue)* sc in next 4 st, *(off-white)* sc in next 8 st, *(petrol blue)* sc in next 14 st [48]
Rnd 15 – 17: *(petrol blue)* sc in next 14 st, *(off-white)* sc in next 20 st, *(petrol blue)* sc in next 14 st [48]
Continue in petrol blue yarn.
Rnd 18: (sc in next 11 st, inc in next st) repeat 4 times [52]

Sew the beak between rounds 13 and 15. Insert the safety eyes between rounds 14 and 15, about 3 stitches away from the beak. Sew the cheeks below the safety eyes.

Continue in a stripe pattern, alternating 1 round in red and 2 rounds in off-white yarn.

Rnd 19 – 21: sc in all 52 st [52]

Rnd 22: (sc in next 12 st, inc in next st) repeat 4 times [56]

Rnd 23 – 25: sc in all 56 st [56]

Rnd 26: (sc in next 13 st, inc in next st) repeat 4 times [60]

Rnd 27 – 28: sc in all 60 st [60]

Change to greenish gray yarn.

Rnd 29: BLO sc in all 60 st [60]

Rnd 30: (sc in next 9 st, inc in next st) repeat 6 times [66]

Rnd 31 – 44: sc in all 66 st [66]

Rnd 45: (sc in next 9 st, dec) repeat 6 times [60]

Rnd 46 – 47: sc in all 60 st [60]

Rnd 48: (sc in next 8 st, dec) repeat 6 times [54]

Rnd 49 – 51: sc in all 54 st [54]

Do not fasten off.

LEGS

To make the legs, divide the work identifying 12 stitches for the front central space between the legs, 12 stitches for the back and 15 stitches for each leg (you may find it useful to use stitch markers). If the legs don't line up nicely with the head, crochet a few more sc on the body or undo them. Join the first marked stitch for the leg on the back side to the marked stitch on the front side, working a single crochet stitch (this sc will be the first stitch of the leg). Now the stitches of the first leg are joined in the round. Continue working the first leg:

Rnd 52: sc in all 15 st [15]

Fasten off, leaving a long tail for sewing. Do not close the leg. Stuff the body and leg firmly.

SECOND LEG

Rejoin the greenish gray yarn in the thirteenth unworked stitch at the back of round 51. This is where we start the first stitch of the second leg. Leave a long starting yarn tail.

Rnd 52: sc in next 15 st. When you reach the 15th stitch of the leg, sc in first st to join the round [15]

Fasten off, leaving a long tail for sewing. Do not close the leg. Add more stuffing if needed.

Using a tapestry needle and the starting yarn tail, sew the 12 stitches between the legs closed.

FEET

(make 2, in yellow yarn)

Rnd 1: start 5 sc in a magic ring [5]

Rnd 2: sc in all 5 st [5]

Rnd 3: inc in all 5 st [10]

Rnd 4: sc in all 10 st [10]

Rnd 5: (sc in next st, inc in next st) repeat 5 times [15]

Rnd 6: sc in all 15 st [15]

Rnd 7: (sc in next 2 st, inc in next st) repeat 5 times [20]

Rnd 8 – 11: sc in all 20 st [20]

Fasten off, leaving a long tail for sewing. Do not stuff. Flatten and, using a tapestry needle, close the opening of the last round. Sew the feet to the legs.

FLIPPERS

(make 2, in petrol blue)
Rnd 1: start 6 sc in a magic ring [6]
Rnd 2: sc in all 6 st [6]
Rnd 3: (sc in next 2 st, inc in next st) repeat 2 times [8]
Rnd 4 – 5: sc in all 8 st [8]
Rnd 6: (sc in next 3 st, inc in next st) repeat 2 times [10]
Rnd 7 – 8: sc in all 10 st [10]
Rnd 9: (sc in next 4 st, inc in next st) repeat 2 times [12]
Rnd 10 – 11: sc in all 12 st [12]
Rnd 12: (sc in next 5 st, inc in next st) repeat 2 times [14]
Rnd 13 – 14: sc in all 14 st [14]
Rnd 15: (sc in next 6 st, inc in next st) repeat 2 times [16]
Rnd 16 – 17: sc in all 16 st [16]
Rnd 18: (sc in next 7 st, inc in next st) repeat 2 times [18]
Rnd 19 – 20: sc in all 18 st [18]
Fasten off, leaving a long tail for sewing. Do not stuff. Flatten and sew the flippers to both sides between rounds 20 and 21.

RAIN CAPE

The hooded rain cape is made of 2 separate parts that are sewn together.

Note: Both the hood and cape are crocheted in half double slip stitch (BLO). If you're not used to this stitch (I'm not), it's a good idea to track the rows.
Note: The rain cape is a small fit, as if Humboldt has outgrown it. If you want to make a bigger rain cape, you can start with either 18 or 21 ch on the hood and make more rows on the cape.

HOOD
(in yellow, using a size E-4 / 3.5 mm crochet hook)
Ch 15. The first row is worked around both sides of the foundation chain. Then crochet hdslst in rows.
Row 1: start in second ch from the hook, hdslst in next 13 st, 3 hdslst in last st. Continue on the other side of the foundation chain, hdslst in next 14 st, ch 1, turn [30]
Row 2 – 13: BLO hdslst in all 30 st, ch 1, turn [30]
Row 14: slst in all 30 st [30]
Fasten off, leaving a long tail for sewing.

CAPE
(in yellow, using a size E-4 / 3.5 mm crochet hook)

Ch 19. Crochet in rows. Work the first row in the back ridge of the foundation chain.

Row 1: inserting the hook in the back bump of the second ch, slst in next 5 st, hdslst in next 13 st, ch 1, turn [18]

Row 2: work this row in BLO, hdslst in next 13 st, slst in next 5 st, ch 1, turn [18]

Row 3: work this row in BLO, slst in next 5 st, hdslst in next 13 st, ch 1, turn [18]

Row 4 – 62: repeat rows 2 and 3.

Fasten off and weave in the yarn ends.

ASSEMBLY
Identify the center of both the hood and the long side of the cape. The slst on the cape create the collar and thus the top side. Count 5 stitches from the top of the cape (where the hdslst begin) and fold the cape downward. Position and pin the hood on this line and stretch the hood so that there are only 9 stitches remaining on each side of the cape. Sew the hood to the cape.

STRAPS
Insert your hook in a stitch on the second row of the cape, right next to the beginning of the collar, with the wrong side of the rain cape facing you, and draw up a loop of yellow yarn. Ch 27. Start in second ch from the hook, slst in next 26 st. Fasten off and weave in the yarn ends. Make a second strap on the other side in the same way.

Tina Lemur

Tina was born in Madagascar, the fourth largest island in the world, and one of the most unique. She descends from a family of doctors and nurses. When Tina was a little lemur, she met Lupita Spider Monkey and Otis Sloth. They became the closest friends and spent many nights staring at the sky. But eventually she went her own way, dedicating her life to her family's passion, giving care to whoever needs it, regardless of size or species. Nowadays, Tina works as a nanny. She adores being with kids, fooling around (and taking care of them, of course). She's also studying to be a nurse just like her grandfather and her aunty. And although she doesn't have the chance to see her friends as often as she would like, Lupita and Otis call her almost every night to jointly look at the night sky.

GALLERY: Scan or visit *www.amigurumi.com/4108* to share pictures and find inspiration.

Size:
14 inches / 36 cm tall when made with the indicated yarn (ears included)

Materials:
– Worsted weight yarn in
  · light warm gray
  · off-white
  · graphite gray
  · dark warm gray
  · yellow
  · subtle green
  · mustard yellow
  · cream
– Size C-2 / 2.75 mm crochet hook
– Black safety eyes (10 mm)
– Tapestry needle
– Fiberfill

Skills needed: magic ring *(page 32)*, changing color mid-round *(page 35)*, changing color at the beginning of a round *(page 35)*, joining parts *(page 39)*, block stitch *(explained in pattern)*, crab stitch *(page 30)*, embroidery *(page 38)*

Note: The head and body are worked in one piece.

CHEEKS

(make 2, in yellow)
Rnd 1: start 8 sc in a magic ring [8]
Slst in next st. Fasten off, leaving a long tail for sewing.

SNOUT

(in graphite gray)
Rnd 1: start 6 sc in a magic ring [6]
Rnd 2: inc in all 6 st [12]
Rnd 3 – 4: sc in all 12 st [12]
Rnd 5: sc in next 2 st, inc in next 4 st, sc in next 6 st [16]
Rnd 6: sc in next 5 st, inc in next 3 st, sc in next 8 st [19]
Fasten off, leaving a long tail for sewing. Embroider the nose and mouth with dark warm gray yarn.

HEAD AND BODY

(start in graphite gray)
Rnd 1: start 6 sc in a magic ring [6]
Rnd 2: inc in all 6 st [12]
Rnd 3: (sc in next st, inc in next st) repeat 6 times [18]
Rnd 4: (sc in next st, inc in next st) repeat 9 times [27]
Rnd 5: (sc in next 2 st, inc in next st) repeat 9 times [36]
Rnd 6: (sc in next 3 st, inc in next st) repeat 9 times [45]
Rnd 7: (sc in next 4 st, inc in next st) repeat 9 times [54]
Rnd 8: (sc in next 8 st, inc in next st) repeat 6 times [60]
Rnd 9 – 11: sc in all 60 st [60]
Change to off-white yarn.
Rnd 12: sc in all 60 st [60]
Continue working with alternating yarns (off-white and dark warm gray). The color you work with is indicated before each part.
Rnd 13: *(off-white)* sc in next 17 st, *(dark warm gray)* sc in next 9 st, *(off-white)* sc in next 8 st, *(dark warm gray)* sc in next 9 st, *(off-white)* sc in next 17 st [60]
Rnd 14 – 18: *(off-white)* sc in next 19 st,

(dark warm gray) sc in next 8 st, (off-white) sc in next 6 st, (dark warm gray) sc in next 8 st, (off-white) sc in next 19 st [60]

Rnd 19: (off-white) sc in next 20 st, (dark warm gray) sc in next 6 st, (off-white) sc in next 8 st, (dark warm gray) sc in next 6 st, (off-white) sc in next 20 st [60]

Continue in off-white yarn.

Rnd 20 – 21: sc in all 60 st [60]

Rnd 22: (sc in next 3 st, dec) repeat 12 times [48]

Rnd 23: (sc in next 2 st, dec) repeat 12 times [36]

Rnd 24: (sc in next 4 st, dec) repeat 6 times [30]

Sew the snout between rounds 13 and 20, in the off-white space between the dark warm gray patches. Stuff the snout with fiberfill before closing the seam. Insert the safety eyes between rounds 16 and 17 about 2 stitches away from the snout. Sew the cheeks behind the safety eyes.

Rnd 25: (sc in next st, dec) repeat 10 times [20]

Continue working with alternating yarns (off-white and light warm gray). The color you work with is indicated before each part.

Note: The off-white patch on the chest should be aligned with the face.

Rnd 26: (light warm gray) sc in next 9 st, (off-white) sc in next 5 st, (light warm gray) sc in next 6 st [20]

Stuff the head firmly with fiberfill.

Rnd 27: (light warm gray) (sc in next st, inc in next st) repeat 4 times, sc in next st, (off-white) (inc in next st, sc in next st) repeat 2 times, inc in next st, (light warm gray) (sc in next st, inc in next st) repeat 3 times [30]

Rnd 28: (light warm gray) sc in next 14 st, (off-white) sc in next 6 st, (light warm gray) sc in next 10 st [30]

Continue in light warm gray yarn.

Rnd 29: (sc in next 4 st, inc in next st) repeat 6 times [36]

Rnd 30 – 46: sc in all 36 st [36]

Rnd 47: (sc in next 4 st, dec) repeat 6 times [30]

Rnd 48: (sc in next 3 st, dec) repeat 6 times [24]

Stuff the body firmly.

Rnd 49: (sc in next 2 st, dec) repeat 6 times [18]

Rnd 50: (sc in next st, dec) repeat 6 times [12]

Rnd 51: dec 6 times [6]

Fasten off, leaving a long tail. Using a tapestry needle, weave the yarn tail through the front loop of each remaining stitch and pull tight to close. Weave in the yarn end.

EARS

(make 2, in off-white)

Rnd 1: start 6 sc in a magic ring [6]

Rnd 2: (sc in next st, inc in next st) repeat 3 times [9]

Rnd 3: (sc in next 2 st, inc in next st) repeat 3 times [12]

Rnd 4: sc in all 12 st [12]

Rnd 5: (sc in next st, inc in next st) repeat 6 times [18]

Rnd 6 – 9: sc in all 18 st [18]

Fasten off, leaving a long tail for sewing. Embroider graphite gray stripes on the inside of the ears. Flatten them before sewing. The ears do not need to be stuffed. Sew the ears to the head.

LEGS

(make 2, start in graphite gray)

Rnd 1: start 5 sc in a magic ring [5]

Rnd 2: inc in all 5 st [10]

Rnd 3 – 7: sc in all 10 st [10]

Rnd 8: (sc in next 4 st, inc in next st) repeat 2 times [12]

Rnd 9 – 11: sc in all 12 st [12]

Stuff lightly with fiberfill and continue stuffing as you go.

Rnd 12: (sc in next 5 st, inc in next st) repeat 2 times [14]

Rnd 13: sc in all 14 st [14]

Work with alternating yarns in the next round, making one stitch in graphite gray and one stitch in light warm gray yarn.

Rnd 14: sc in all 14 st [14]
Change to light warm gray yarn.
Rnd 15 – 35: sc in all 14 st [14]
Rnd 36: (sc in next 5 st, dec) repeat 2 times [12]
Fasten off, leaving a long tail for sewing. Add more stuffing if needed.

TOES
(in graphite gray)
Insert the hook into a stitch of round 2 and draw up a loop of graphite gray yarn.
Crochet in rows.
Row 1: (Ch 6, start in second ch from the hook, slst in next 5 st, slst in next st on the leg) repeat 4 times [4 toes]
Fasten off and weave in the yarn ends. Sew the legs to the body between rounds 45 and 46.

ARMS

(make 2, start in off-white)
Rnd 1: start 5 sc in a magic ring [5]
Rnd 2: inc in all 5 st [10]
Rnd 3 – 8: sc in all 10 st [10]
Rnd 9: (sc in next 4 st, inc in next st) repeat 2 times [12]
Stuff lightly with fiberfill and continue stuffing as you go. Work with alternating yarns in the next round, making one stitch in off-white and one stitch in light warm gray yarn.
Rnd 10: sc in all 12 st [12]
Change to light warm gray yarn.
Rnd 11 – 26: sc in all 12 st [12]
Rnd 27: (sc in next st, dec) repeat 4 times [8]
Fasten off, leaving a long tail for sewing. Add more stuffing if needed.

FINGERS
(in off-white)
Insert the hook into a stitch of round 2 and draw up a loop of off-white yarn.
Crochet in rows.
Row 1: (Ch 6, start in second ch from the hook, slst in next 5 st, slst in next st on the arm) repeat 3 times [3 fingers]

Fasten off and weave in the yarn ends.
Sew the arms to both sides between rounds 28 and 29.

TAIL

(start in graphite gray)
Rnd 1: start 6 sc in a magic ring [6]
Rnd 2: inc in all 6 st [12]
Rnd 3: (sc in next st, inc in next st) repeat 6 times [18]
Rnd 4 – 10: sc in all 18 st [18]
Continue working in a stripe pattern, alternating 3 rounds in off-white and 3 rounds in graphite gray yarn.
Rnd 11: (sc in next 7 st, dec) repeat 2 times [16]
Stuff lightly with fiberfill and continue stuffing as you go.
Rnd 12 – 25: sc in all 16 st [16]
Rnd 26: (sc in next 6 st, dec) repeat 2 times [14]
Rnd 27 – 40: sc in all 14 st [14]
Rnd 41: (sc in next 5 st, dec) repeat 2 times [12]
Rnd 42 – 52: sc in all 12 st [12]
Fasten off, leaving a long tail for sewing. Add more stuffing if needed. Sew the tail to the back, centered over rounds 45 and 46.

DRESS

The dress is made with 2 squares that are joined together.

SQUARE
(make 2, start in subtle green yarn)
Ch 34. Crochet in rows.
Note: We work the block stitch by working 2 rows in the same direction: 1 row in double crochet and 1 row crocheting in the spaces between the dc-stitches. Pay attention to the "right" and "wrong" side of the work.
Note: Count the ch 3 we skip at the beginning as your first dc stitch.
Row 1 (right side): start in fourth ch from the hook, dc in next 31 st [32] Mark the last stitch.
Do not fasten off. Do not turn your work and keep your work with the right side facing you.
Note: In the next row, we'll work in the spaces between the

dc stitches of row 1.

Row 2: (right side): draw up a loop of cream yarn in the first space between the skipped 3 ch and the first dc, sc in this space, (ch 2, skip next 2 dc-spaces, sc in next dc-space) repeat 10 times. Mark the last stitch.
Do not fasten off. Turn your work.

Row 3 (wrong side): remove the stitch marker you added at the end of row 1, continue with the subtle green yarn, ch 3, (3 dc in ch-2 space of row 2) repeat 10 times, dc in the space between the sc and the ch 3 you made at the beginning of row 1. Mark the last stitch.
Do not fasten off. Do not turn your work and keep your work with the wrong side facing you.

Row 4 (wrong side): remove the stitch marker you added at the end of row 2, continue with the cream yarn, ch 2, sc into the space between the ch 3 and the first dc, (ch 2, sc into next space between the 3-dc-clusters) repeat 9 times, ch 2, sc into the space between the final 3-dc-cluster and the final dc of row 3. Mark the last stitch.
Do not fasten off. Turn your work.

Row 5 (right side): remove the stitch marker you added at the end of row 3, continue with the subtle green yarn, ch 3, (3 dc into ch-2 space of row 4) repeat 10 times, dc into the space between the sc and the ch 3 you made at the beginning of row 3. Mark the last stitch.
Do not fasten off. Do not turn your work and keep your work with the right side facing you.

Row 6 (right side): remove the stitch marker you added at the end of row 4, continue with the cream yarn, ch 2, sc into the space between the ch 3 and the first dc, (ch 2, sc into next space between the 3-dc-clusters) repeat 9 times, ch 2, sc into the space between the final 3-dc-cluster and the final dc of row 5. Mark the last stitch.

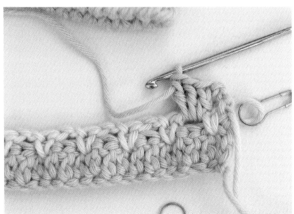

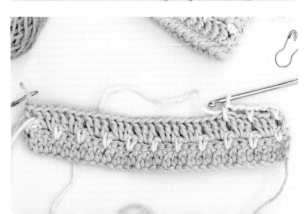

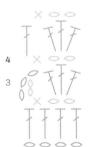

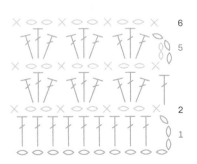

Do not fasten off. Turn your work.
Row 7: repeat row 3
Row 8: repeat row 4.
Fasten off the cream yarn.
Row 9: repeat row 5.
Pull up a loop of mustard yellow yarn in the last cream sc stitch of Row 8.
Row 10: repeat row 6 with mustard yellow yarn.
Row 11: repeat row 3 with subtle green yarn
Row 12: repeat row 4 with mustard yellow yarn.
Row 13: repeat row 5 with subtle green yarn.
Row 14: repeat row 6 with mustard yellow yarn.
Row 15: repeat row 3 with subtle green yarn.
Row 16: repeat row 4 with mustard yellow yarn.
Row 17: repeat row 5 with subtle green yarn.
Fasten off. Weave in the mustard yellow yarn tail and leave a long subtle green yarn tail.

ASSEMBLY
Start by sewing the top part. Place the squares with the right side facing up and row 17 of both pieces touching each other. In row 17, mark the 8 outer stitches for each shoulder and 16 center stitches for the collar (the starting chain in row 17 counts as the first dc stitch, giving you 32 stitches in total).
You can use stitch markers to help hold your work together.
We will join the pieces with the flat slip stitch seam technique. Using the remaining subtle green yarn tail, insert the hook from front to back into the back loop of the right corner stitch of the first square. Draw up a loop of subtle green yarn.
Hold the yarn tail underneath the pieces you're joining (and keep it underneath your work while joining the squares). Then, insert the hook from top to bottom into the back loop of the corner stitch of the second square. Draw up a loop of subtle green yarn and draw it through all loops on the hook to complete the first slip stitch.
Insert the hook from front to back into the next back loop of the first square and the next back loop of the second square. Draw up a loop of subtle green yarn and draw it through all loops on the hook to complete the slip stitch.
Repeat this until you have made 8 slst for the first shoulder. Fasten off and weave in the yarn ends.

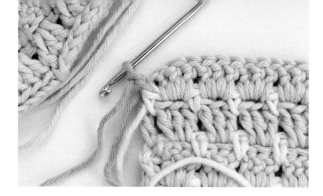
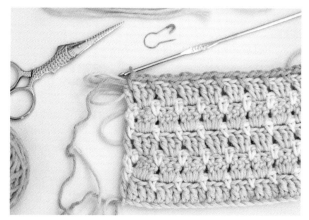

Join the squares on the other side (for the other shoulder) in the same way.
To join the sides of the dress, fold the dress inside out and hold it with the wrong sides facing up. Line up the row-ends and, using a tapestry needle, sew the edges together from row 1 to 9 (where the first row in mustard yellow yarn begins). Sew the other side in the same way. The remaining holes are the armholes.

COLLAR
(in subtle green)
Join the subtle green yarn in the first stitch next to the shoulder seam of row 17. Slst in next 16 st, 2 slst in the side of the shoulder seam, slst in next 16 st, 2 slst in the side of the shoulder seam [36]
Fasten off and weave in the yarn ends.

SLEEVES
(in subtle green)
Join the subtle green yarn in a row-end at the bottom center of the armhole.
Rnd 1: ch 3, make 26 dc around the armhole, slst in third ch [27]
Rnd 2: slst in all 27 st [27]
Fasten off and weave in the yarn ends.
Make the second sleeve in the same way.

BOTTOM EDGE
(in subtle green)
Join the subtle green yarn in row 1, at the bottom of the dress.
Rnd 1: insert the hook in the spaces between the dc stitches of row 1, sc in next 64 st [64]
Rnd 2: ch 1, crab stitch in all 64 st [64]
Fasten off and weave in the yarn ends.

Ramona Cow

Ramona grew up playing with Lucas Fox, so it's no wonder she spent much of her time reading detective and mystery novels (and watching 'Back To The Future' more times than any being she has ever met - and she met a lot of people). What she loved most about those stories was the part where the characters searched for clues and connected the dots to find the truth. She started doing her own investigations in the neighborhood, researching unsolved mysteries - such as who had eaten the last cupcake of Eduardo Cutesaurus' auntie or where did Angus Squirrel hide his food for winter. Now, Ramona is an accomplished investigative journalist who writes in-depth stories for major newspapers.

 SKILL LEVEL ***

GALLERY: Scan or visit *www.amigurumi.com/4109* to share pictures and find inspiration.

Size:
14 inches / 35 cm tall when made with the indicated yarn (horns included)

Materials:
– Worsted weight yarn in
 · brown
 · pastel pink
 · pale pink
 · turmeric yellow
 · cream
 · black (leftover)
 · graphite gray
 · pastel mint
– optional: fingering weight yarn in
 · pastel mint
– Size C-2 / 2.75 mm crochet hook
– optional: size 2.00 mm crochet hook
– Black safety eyes (10 mm)
– Tapestry needle
– Fiberfill

Skills needed: magic ring (page 32), working around a foundation chain (page 34), changing color at the beginning of a round (page 35), dividing the body in two parts (page 47), working in the back ridge of a chain (page 20), half double slip stitch (page 26), mattress stitch (explained In pattern), flat slip stitch seam (page 94), joining parts (page 39), embroidery (page 38)

CHEEKS

(make 2, in pastel pink)
Rnd 1: start 8 sc in a magic ring [8]
Slst in next st. Fasten off, leaving a long tail for sewing.

HEAD

(start in pastel pink)
Ch 8. Stitches are worked around both sides of the foundation chain.
Rnd 1: start in second ch from the hook, inc in this st, sc in next 5 st, 4 sc in last st. Continue on the other side of the foundation chain, sc in next 5 st, inc in last st [18]
Rnd 2: inc in next 2 st, sc in next 5 st, inc in next 4 st, sc in next 5 st, inc in next 2 st [26]
Rnd 3: sc in next 2 st, inc in next st, sc in next 8 st, inc in next st, sc in next 3 st, inc in next st, sc in next 8 st, inc in next st, sc in next st [30]
Rnd 4 – 5: sc in all 30 st [30]
Change to cream yarn.
Rnd 6 – 8: sc in all 30 st [30]

Change to brown yarn. Continue working with alternating yarns (brown and cream). The color you work with is indicated before each part.
Note: The cream patch should be positioned in the center of the long side of your crochet work. You might need to add or undo a few brown stitches at the start of round 9 to get to the right position.
Note: In the next rounds you will sometimes read "½ inc in next st". Work the first stitch of this increase in one color and the second stitch in the other color.
Rnd 9: *(brown)* sc in next 5 st, inc in next st, ½ inc in next st, *(cream)* ½ inc in next st, inc in next 2 st, ½ inc in next st, *(brown)* ½ inc in next st, inc in next st, sc in next 19 st [36]
Rnd 10 – 12: *(brown)* sc in next 8 st, *(cream)* sc in next 6 st, *(brown)* sc in next 22 st [36]
Embroider the mouth between rounds 7 and 8 with black yarn.
Rnd 13: *(brown)* sc in next 5 st, inc in next st, sc in next st, inc in next st, *(cream)* (sc in next st, inc in next st) repeat 3 times, *(brown)* sc in next st,

96

inc in next st, sc in next 20 st [42]

Rnd 14 – 15: *(brown)* sc in next 10 st, *(cream)* sc in next 9 st, *(brown)* sc in next 23 st [42]

Rnd 16: *(brown)* sc in next 7 st, inc in next st, sc in next 2 st, *(cream)* (inc in next st, sc in next 2 st) repeat 3 times, ½ inc in next st, *(brown)* ½ inc in next st, sc in next 2 st, inc in next st, sc in next 19 st [48]

Rnd 17: *(brown)* sc in next 11 st, *(cream)* sc in next 13 st, *(brown)* sc in next 24 st [48]

Rnd 18: *(brown)* sc in next 7 st, inc in next st, sc in next 3 st, *(cream)* (inc in next st, sc in next 3 st) repeat 3 times, inc in next st, *(brown)* sc in next 3 st, inc in next st, sc in next 20 st [54]

Rnd 19 – 24: *(brown)* sc in next 12 st, *(cream)* sc in next 17 st, *(brown)* sc in next 25 st [54]

Rnd 25: *(brown)* sc in next 13 st, *(cream)* sc in next 15 st, *(brown)* sc in next 26 st [54]

Rnd 26: *(brown)* sc in next 14 st, *(cream)* sc in next 13 st, *(brown)* sc in next 27 st [54]

Rnd 27: *(brown)* sc in next 15 st, *(cream)* sc in next 11 st, *(brown)* sc in next 28 st [54]

Rnd 28: *(brown)* sc in next 16 st, *(cream)* sc in next 9 st, *(brown)* sc in next 29 st [54]

Change to brown yarn.

Rnd 29: sc in all 54 st [54]

Insert the safety eyes between rounds 21 and 22, about 4 stitches away from the cream patch. Sew the cheeks below the safety eyes.

Rnd 30: (sc in next 7 st, dec) repeat 6 times [48]

Rnd 31: sc in all 48 st [48]

Rnd 32: (sc in next 6 st, dec) repeat 6 times [42]

Rnd 33: (sc in next 5 st, dec) repeat 6 times [36]

Rnd 34: (sc in next 4 st, dec) repeat 6 times [30]

Stuff the head firmly.

Rnd 35: (sc in next 3 st, dec) repeat 6 times [24]

Rnd 36: (sc in next 2 st, dec) repeat 6 times [18]

Rnd 37: (sc in next st, dec) repeat 6 times [12]

Rnd 38: dec 6 times [6]

Fasten off, leaving a long tail. Using a tapestry needle, weave the yarn tail through the front loop of each remaining stitch and pull tight to close. Weave in the yarn end.

BODY

(start in brown)

Leave a long starting yarn tail. Ch 27. Make sure your chain isn't twisted. Insert the hook in the first chain stitch and join the foundation chain with a slst. Continue working in a spiral.

Rnd 1 – 2: sc in all 27 st [27]

Rnd 3: (sc in next 8 st, inc in next st) repeat 3 times [30]

Rnd 4: sc in all 30 st [30]

Rnd 5: (sc in next 4 st, inc in next st) repeat 6 times [36]

Rnd 6 – 7: sc in all 36 st [36]

Rnd 8: (sc in next 5 st, inc in next st) repeat 6 times [42]

Rnd 9 – 12: sc in all 42 st [42]

Rnd 13: (sc in next 6 st, inc in next st) repeat 6 times [48]

Rnd 14 – 22: sc in all 48 st [48]

Rnd 23: (sc in next 10 st, dec) repeat 4 times [44]

Rnd 24 – 25: sc in all 44 st [44]

Rnd 26: (sc in next 9 st, dec) repeat 4 times [40]

Rnd 27: sc in all 40 st [40]

Do not fasten off.

LEGS

To make the legs, divide the work identifying 4 stitches for the front central space between the legs, 4 stitches for the back and 16 stitches for each leg (you may find it useful to use stitch markers). Join the first marked stitch for the leg on the back side to the marked stitch on the front side, working a single crochet stitch (this sc will be the first stitch of the leg). Now the stitches of the first leg are joined in the round. Continue working the first leg:

Rnd 28 – 47: sc in all 16 st [16]

Change to cream yarn.

Rnd 48 – 49: sc in all 16 st [16]

Change to graphite gray yarn.

Rnd 50 – 52: sc in all 16 st [16]

Stuff the body and leg. Do not overstuff, so you can work the hooves more easily. Make sure your hook is positioned in the center of the hoof. If necessary, crochet a few more sc or undo a few to correct your position. Next, skip 8 st and join to ninth stitch with a

sc. This sc will be the first stitch of the next round.
Rnd 53 – 54: sc in all 8 st [8]
Stuff the toe lightly.
Rnd 55: dec 4 times [4]
Fasten off, leaving a long tail. Using a tapestry needle, weave the yarn tail through the front loop of each remaining stitch and pull tight to close. Weave in the yarn end. Rejoin the graphite gray yarn in the first unworked stitch next to the first toe and repeat Rnd 53-55 to make the second toe.

SECOND LEG
Rejoin the brown yarn in the fifth unworked stitch at the back of round 27. This is where we start the first stitch of the second leg. Leave a long starting yarn tail.
Rnd 28: sc in next 16 st. When you reach the 16th stitch of the leg, sc in first st to join the round [16]
Rnd 29 – 55: repeat the pattern for the first leg.
Add more stuffing if needed. Using a tapestry needle and the starting yarn tail, sew the 4 stitches between the legs closed. Sew the body between rounds 21 and 29 of the head.

ARMS

(make 2, start in graphite gray)
Rnd 1: start 6 sc in a magic ring [6]
Rnd 2: inc in all 6 st [12]
Rnd 3 – 7: sc in all 12 st [12]
Change to brown yarn.
Rnd 8 – 26: sc in all 12 st [12]
Rnd 27: (sc in next st, dec) repeat 4 times [8]
Fasten off, leaving a long tail for sewing. Stuff with fiberfill. Sew the arms to both sides between rounds 3 and 4.

HORNS

(make 2, in cream)
Rnd 1: start 6 sc in a magic ring [6]
Rnd 2: sc in all 6 st [6]
Rnd 3: inc in next 2 st, sc in next 4 st [8]
Rnd 4: sc in all 8 st [8]
Rnd 5: (sc in next st, inc in next st) repeat 2 times, sc in next 4 st [10]
Rnd 6: sc in all 10 st [10]
Rnd 7: sc in next 2 st, inc in next st, sc in next st, inc in next st, sc in next 5 st [12]
Rnd 8: dec, sc in next 2 st, inc in next st, sc in next st, inc in next st, sc in next 3 st, dec [12]
Rnd 9: sc in all 12 st [12]
Fasten off, leaving a long tail for sewing. Stuff lightly. Sew the horns to the top of the head, between rounds 26 and 30, next to the cream patch.

OUTER EARS

(make 2, in brown)
Rnd 1: start 6 sc in a magic ring [6]
Rnd 2: inc in all 6 st [12]
Rnd 3: sc in all 12 st [12]
Rnd 4: (sc in next 3 st, inc in next st) repeat 3 times [15]
Rnd 5: sc in all 15 st [15]

Rnd 6: (sc in next 4 st, inc in next st) repeat 3 times [18]
Rnd 7: sc in all 18 st [18]
Rnd 8: (sc in next 5 st, inc in next st) repeat 3 times [21]
Rnd 9: sc in all 21 st [21]
Rnd 10: (sc in next 6 st, inc in next st) repeat 3 times [24]
Rnd 11: sc in all 24 st [24]
Rnd 12: (sc in next 7 st, inc in next st) repeat 3 times [27]
Rnd 13 – 16: sc in all 27 st [27]
Rnd 17: (sc in next 7 st, dec) repeat 3 times [24]
Rnd 18: (sc in next 2 st, dec) repeat 6 times [18]
Rnd 19: sc in all 18 st [18]
Rnd 20: (sc in next 4 st, dec) repeat 3 times [15]
Rnd 21 – 22: sc in all 15 st [15]
Fasten off, leaving a long tail for sewing. Do not stuff.

INNER EARS

(make 2, in pastel pink)
Ch 11. Stitches are worked around both sides of the
foundation chain.
Rnd 1: start in second ch from the hook, inc in this st,
sc in next 8 st, 3 sc in last st. Continue on the other side
of the foundation chain, sc in next 9 st [22]
Fasten off, leaving a long tail for sewing. Sew the inner
ear to the center of the inside of the brown ear. Flatten
and pinch the ears. Sew the bottom 3 stitches together.
Sew the ears to the head, below the horns, between
rounds 26 and 29.

HAIR

(in cream)
Note: Every time I make Ramona Cow I crochet her a
different hairdo, so you can play around and do as many
hair strands as you like. She even looks gorgeous without
her fringe.
Insert the hook in round 23 of the head, into the cream
patch, about 5 stitches away from the brown yarn.
Row 1: (ch 4, start in second ch from the hook, slst in next
3 st, slst in next stitch on the head) repeat 7 times [7 hair
strands]

Turn the head and continue working in round 24 of the head.
Row 2: (ch 4, start in second ch from the hook, slst in next 3 st, slst in next stitch on the head) repeat 9 times [9 hair strands]
Turn the head and continue working in round 25 of the head.
Row 3: (ch 4, start in second ch from the hook, slst in next 3 st, slst in next stitch on the head) repeat 9 times [9 hair strands]
Turn the head and continue working in round 26 of the head.
Row 4: (ch 4, start in second ch from the hook, slst in next 3 st, slst in next stitch on the head) repeat 7 times [7 hair strands]
Turn the head and continue working in round 27 of the head.
Row 5: (ch 4, start in second ch from the hook, slst in next 3 st, slst in next stitch on the head) repeat 7 times [7 hair strands]
Fasten off and weave in the yarn ends.

JUMPSUIT

The jumpsuit is made with two rectangles that are sewn together.

RECTANGLE
(make 2, in pastel mint)
Ch 33. Crochet in rows.
Row 1: start in second ch from hook, slst in next 8 st, hdslst in next 18 st, slst in next 6 st, ch 1, turn [32]
Row 2: work this row in BLO, slst in next 6 st, hdslst in next 18 st, slst in next 8 st, ch 1, turn [32]
Row 3: work this row in BLO, slst in next 8 st, hdslst in next 18 st, slst in next 6 st, ch 1, turn [32]
Row 4 – 27: repeat rows 2-3
Fasten off, leaving a long tail for sewing.
Fold the first rectangle lengthwise in half, with the right side facing outward. Using a tapestry needle and the leftover yarn tail, sew the section of 6 slst of Row 1 and 27 together to create the first leg opening. Repeat for the second rectangle. Then, line up the open edge of both rectangles. Sew next 18 hdslst (for the jumpsuit) together, then sew next 8 slst (for the waistband) together. Repeat this for the remaining open edge at the back side.
Note: I used the mattress stitch for sewing, but you can use any sewing technique. Grab a strand of yarn from each edge, alternating back and forth. Insert the needle from top to bottom through the top loop on one side, then insert the needle from top to bottom through the bottom loop on the other side.

SHOULDER STRAPS
(make 2, in pastel mint)
Leave a long starting yarn tail. Ch 27. Crochet in rows.
Row 1: start in second ch from the hook, slst in next 26 st, ch 1, turn [26]
Row 2: BLO slst in all 26 st [26]
You can fasten off at this point or make one of the following edgings.

EDGING OPTION A
(making the shell stitch)
Ch 1, turn. Crochet in rows.
Row 3: sc in next st, (skip 1 st, 5 dc in next st, skip 1 st, slst in next st) repeat 6 times, sc in last st.
Fasten off, leaving a tail for sewing. Repeat for the other shoulder strap.

EDGING OPTION B
(making ruffles, using fingering weight yarn and a 2.00 mm crochet hook)
Draw up a loop of fingering weight yarn in the first stitch of the shoulder strap. Crochet in rows.
Row 3: inc in all 26 st, ch 2, turn [52]
Row 4: (hdc in next st, hdc inc in next st) repeat 26 times, ch 1, turn [78]
Row 5: slst in all 78 st [78]
Fasten off, leaving a tail for sewing. Repeat for the other shoulder strap.

OPTION A   OPTION B

Sew the straps to the front and back of the jumpsuit, covering the top of the waistband.

CARDIGAN

The cardigan is made with two hexagons that are folded and crocheted or sewn together (I include both options).
Note: Count the ch 3 at the beginning as 1 dc. Count the ch 2 at the beginning as 1 hdc.
Note: Crochet in joined rounds.

HEXAGONS
(make 2, start in yellow)
Rnd 1: start in a magic ring: ch 3, 2 dc, ch 1, (3 dc, ch 1) repeat 5 times, slst in third starting ch to join the round [18 + 6 ch]
Change to cream yarn.
Rnd 2: ch 3, dc in next 2 st, 2 dc + ch 2 + 2 dc in next ch-1 space, (dc in next 3 st, 2 dc + ch 2 + 2 dc in next ch-1 space) repeat 5 times, slst in third starting ch to join the round [42 + 12 ch]
Change to turmeric yellow yarn.
Rnd 3: ch 3, dc in next 4 st, 2 dc + ch 2 + 2 dc in next ch-2 space, (dc in next 7 st, 2 dc + ch 2 + 2 dc in next ch-2 space) repeat 5 times, dc in next 2 st, slst in third starting ch to join the round [66 + 12 ch]
Note: Do not worry if you start to see creases, these are the result of the large number of stitches and will create the cardigan's sleeves.
Change to cream yarn.
Rnd 4: ch 3, dc in next 6 st, 2 dc + ch 2 + 2 dc in next ch-2 space, (dc in next 11 st, 2 dc + ch 2 + 2 dc in next ch-2 space) repeat 5 times, dc in next 4 st, slst in third starting ch to join the round [90 + 12 ch]
Change to turmeric yellow yarn.
Rnd 5: ch 2, hdc in next 8 st, 2 hdc + ch 2 + 2 hdc in next ch-2 space, (hdc in next 15 st, 2 hdc + ch 2 + 2 hdc in next ch-2 space) repeat 5 times, hdc in next 6 st, slst in second starting ch to join the round [114 + 12 ch]
Fasten off and weave in the yarn ends.

ASSEMBLY
Fold one hexagon in half and hold the points together with a stitch marker. You will have an L-shape when folded. Repeat for the other hexagon. Line up the straight side of the hexagons as shown in the pictures. Join on one side, either by using a crochet hook (using the flat slip stitch seam technique) or by sewing them together with a tapestry needle, using the mattress stitch.
Then, join the shoulders. Mark 16 stitches for each shoulder and sew them together.

EDGING
(in pale pink)
With the right side facing up, insert the hook at the front of the neckline, left shoulder.
Note: Your total stitch count might vary in these rounds, based on whether you've sewn/crocheted these pieces together.
Rnd 1: slst in next 4 st, 2 sc in next ch-2-space, sc in next 19/20 st, 2 sc in next ch-2-space, sc in next 42/43 st, 2 sc in next ch-2-space, sc in next 20 st, 2 sc in next ch-2-space, slst in next 17/18 st (neckline) [approx. 114]
Rnd 2: BLO slst in all 114 st [114]
Fasten off and weave in the yarn ends.

SLEEVE CUFFS (in pale pink)
Join pale pink yarn in a bottom center stitch of the sleeve.
Note: Your total stitch count might vary in these rounds, based on whether you've sewn/crocheted these pieces together.
Rnd 1: sc in all st [22/23]
Rnd 2: BLO slst in all st [22/23]
Fasten off and weave in the yarn ends. Work the second sleeve cuff in the same way.

Peggy Hippopotamus

Peggy is a costume designer. She creates outfits and accessories for film and stage actors. Period dramas were her favorite plays when she was a tiny little hippo, but when Peggy coincidentally landed a job working in sci-fi in a major Hollywood studio (a story I'll tell another time), she found her creative purpose: imagining how beings in other worlds, times and universes would dress, how they would adapt to new environments and what their clothes would mean in their societies. She's aware she has a super important job, because costumes identify a character as much as the actor who plays the part. Imagine Indiana Jones without his iconic hat, or Leia Organa without her dress and hairdo.

GALLERY: Scan or visit www.amigurumi.com/4110 to share pictures and find inspiration.

HEAD

(in mink brown)
Ch 8. Stitches are worked around both sides of the foundation chain.
Rnd 1: start in second ch from the hook, inc in this st, sc in next 5 st, 4 sc in last st. Continue on the other side of the foundation chain, sc in next 5 st, inc in last st [18]
Rnd 2: inc in next 2 st, sc in next 5 st, inc in next 4 st, sc in next 5 st, inc in next 2 st [26]
Rnd 3: (sc in next st, inc in next st) repeat 2 times, sc in next 6 st, (inc in next st, sc in next st) repeat 3 times, inc in next st, sc in next 6 st, inc in next st, sc in next st, inc in next st [34]
Rnd 4: (sc in next 2 st, inc in next st) repeat 2 times, sc in next 7 st, (inc in next st, sc in next 2 st) repeat 3 times, inc in next st, sc in next 7 st, inc in next st, sc in next 2 st, inc in next st [42]
Rnd 5 – 7: sc in all 42 st [42]
Note: In round 8 you add the hippo's nostrils. Check if they're aligned at an equal distance from the center and correct if necessary.
Rnd 8: sc in next 6 st, 5-dc-bobble in next st, sc in next 8 st, 5-dc-bobble in next st, sc in next 26 st [42]
Rnd 9 – 15: sc in all 42 st [42]
Rnd 16: (inc in next st, sc in next 2 st) repeat 7 times, inc in next st, sc in next 20 st [50]
Rnd 17: sc in all 50 st [50]
Rnd 18: sc in next 8 st, (inc in next st, sc in next st) repeat 7 times, inc in next st, sc in next 27 st [58]
Rnd 19 – 30: sc in all 58 st [58]
Rnd 31: (dec, sc in next 10 st) repeat 3 times, dec, sc in next 20 st [54]
Rnd 32: sc in all 54 st [54]
Insert the safety eyes between rounds 22 and 23, with an interspace of about 24 stitches. Embroider cheeks below the eyes with pastel pink yarn.
Rnd 33: (sc in next 7 st, dec) repeat 6 times [48]
Rnd 34: (sc in next 6 st, dec) repeat 6 times [42]
Rnd 35: (sc in next 5 st, dec) repeat 6 times [36]
Rnd 36: (sc in next 4 st, dec) repeat 6 times [30]
Stuff the head firmly.
Rnd 37: (sc in next 3 st, dec) repeat 6 times [24]
Rnd 38: (sc in next 2 st, dec) repeat 6 times [18]
Rnd 39: (sc in next st, dec) repeat 6 times [12]
Rnd 40: dec 6 times [6]
Fasten off, leaving a long tail. Using a tapestry needle, weave the yarn tail through the front loop of each remaining stitch and pull tight to close. Weave in the yarn end.

BODY

(start in mink brown)
Leave a long starting yarn tail. Ch 30.
Make sure your chain isn't twisted. Insert
the hook in the first chain stitch and join
the foundation chain with a slst. Continue
working in a spiral.
Rnd 1 – 2: sc in all 30 st [30]
Continue working in a jacquard pattern,
alternating off-white and yellow yarn. The
color you work is indicated before each
part.
Note: In the next round you will read ½
inc in next st. Work the first stitch of this
increase in one color and the second
stitch in the other color.
Rnd 3: ((yellow) sc in next 4 st, ½ inc in
next st, (off-white) ½ inc in same st) repeat 6 times [36]
Rnd 4: (off-white) sc in next st, ((yellow)
sc in next 3 st, (off-white) sc in next 3 st)
repeat 5 times, (yellow) sc in next 3 st,
(off-white) sc in next 2 st [36]
Rnd 5: (off-white) (sc in next 5 st, inc in
next st) repeat 6 times [42]
Rnd 6: ((off-white) sc in next 4 st, (yellow)
sc in next 3 st) repeat 6 times [42]
Rnd 7: (off-white) sc in next 3 st, ((yellow)
sc in next 5 st, (off-white) sc in next 2 st)
repeat 5 times, (yellow) sc in next 4 st [42]
Rnd 8: (yellow) sc in next st, ((off-white) sc
in next 2 st, (yellow) sc in next 5 st) repeat
5 times, (off-white) sc in next 2 st, (yellow)
sc in next 4 st [42]
Rnd 9: (yellow) sc in next st, (off-white)
sc in next st, inc in next st, ((yellow) sc in next 5 st,
(off-white) sc in next st, inc in next st) repeat 5 times,
(yellow) sc in next 4 st [48]
Rnd 10: (yellow) sc in next st, (off-white) sc in next
4 st, ((yellow) sc in next 3 st, (off-white) sc in next
5 st) repeat 5 times, (yellow) sc in next 3 st [48]
Rnd 11: (off-white) sc in all 48 st [48]
Rnd 12: (off-white) sc in next st, ((yellow) sc in next
3 st, (off-white) sc in next 5 st) repeat 5 times, (yellow) sc in next 3 st, (off-white) sc in next 4 st [48]
Rnd 13: ((yellow) sc in next 5 st, (off-white) sc in next
st, inc in next st, sc in next st) repeat 5 times, (yellow)
sc in next 5 st, (off-white) sc in next st, inc in next st,
sc in next st [54]
Rnd 14 – 15: ((yellow) sc in next 5 st, (off-white) sc in
next 4 st) repeat 6 times [54]
Rnd 16: (off-white) sc in next st, ((yellow) sc in next
3 st, (off-white) sc in next 6 st) repeat 5 times, (yellow)
sc in next 3 st, (off-white) sc in next 5 st [54]
Rnd 17: (off-white) (sc in next 8 st, inc in next st)
repeat 6 times [60]
Change to mink brown yarn.
Rnd 18: BLO sc in all 60 st [60]
Rnd 19 – 26: sc in all 60 st [60]
Rnd 27: (sc in next 8 st, dec) repeat 6 times [54]
Rnd 28 – 31: sc in all 54 st [54]
Rnd 32: (sc in next 7 st, dec) repeat 6 times [48]
Rnd 33 – 36: sc in all 48 st [48]
Do not fasten off

LEGS

To make the legs, divide the work identifying 4 stitches for the front central space between the legs, 4 stitches for the back and 20 stitches for each leg (you may find it useful to use stitch markers). Join the first marked stitch for the leg on the back side to the marked stitch on the front side, working a single crochet stitch (this sc will be the first stitch of the leg). Now the stitches of the first leg are joined in the round. Continue working the first leg:

Rnd 37 – 46: sc in all 20 st [20]
Stuff the body and leg firmly.
Rnd 47: (sc in next 2 st, dec) repeat 5 times [15]
Rnd 48: (sc in next st, dec) repeat 5 times [10]
Rnd 49: dec 5 times [5]
Fasten off, leaving a long tail. Using a tapestry needle, weave the yarn tail through the front loop of each remaining stitch and pull tight to close. Weave in the yarn end.

SECOND LEG
Rejoin the mink brown yarn in the fifth unworked stitch at the back of round 36. This is where we start the first stitch of the second leg. Leave a long starting yarn tail.
Rnd 37: sc in next 20 st. When you reach the 20th st of the leg, sc in first st to join the round [20]
Rnd 38 – 49: repeat the pattern for the first leg. Stuff the second leg and add more stuffing to the body if needed. Using a tapestry needle and the starting yarn tail, sew the 4 stitches between the legs closed. Sew the body between rounds 19 and 30 of the head.

OUTER EARS

(make 2, in mink brown)
Rnd 1: start 6 sc in a magic ring [6]
Rnd 2: inc in all 6 st [12]
Rnd 3: (sc in next st, inc in next st) repeat 6 times [18]
Rnd 4 – 10: sc in all 18 st [18]
Fasten off, leaving a long tail for sewing.

INNER EARS

(make 2, in pastel pink)
Rnd 1: start 8 sc in a magic ring [8]
Fasten off, leaving a long tail for sewing. Sew the inner ear to the center of the inside of the mink brown ear, between rounds 5 and 8. Flatten and pinch the ears. Sew the bottom 3 stitches together. Sew the ears to the top of the head, over rounds 28 to 32.

ARMS

(make 2, start in mink brown)
Rnd 1: start 5 sc in a magic ring [5]
Rnd 2: inc in all 5 st [10]
Rnd 3: (sc in next st, inc in next st) repeat 5 times [15]
Rnd 4 – 5: sc in all 15 st [15]
Rnd 6: sc in next st, 5-dc-bobble in next st, sc in next 13 st [15]
Rnd 7 – 16: sc in all 15 st [15]
Change to off-white yarn. Continue working in a stripe pattern, alternating 1 round in yellow and 2 rounds in off-white.
Rnd 17 – 22: sc in all 15 st [15]
Rnd 23: (sc in next st, dec) repeat 5 times [10]
Fasten off, leaving a long tail for sewing. Stuff with fiberfill. Sew the arms to both sides between rounds 3 and 4.

TROUSERS

(in subtle green)
The trousers are made with two crochet rectangles that are sewn together.

RECTANGLE
(make 2, in subtle green)
Ch 25. Crochet in rows.
Row 1: start in second ch from the hook, slst in next 6 st, hdslst in next 18 st, ch 1, turn [24]
Row 2: work this row in BLO, hdslst in next 18 st, slst in next 6 st, ch 1, turn [24]
Row 3: work this row in BLO, slst in next 6 st, hdslst in next 18 st, ch 1, turn [24]
Row 4 – 31: repeat rows 2 and 3.
Fasten off, leaving a long tail for sewing.

ASSEMBLY
Line up the edges of both rectangles as shown in the pictures, with the right sides facing outward. Using a tapestry needle, sew the 18 stitches of the rise together (leave the section of 6 slst at the bottom unsewn for now).

Note: I used the mattress stitch for sewing, but you can use any sewing technique.

Turn your work, with the wrong side facing outward. Fold the first rectangle lengthwise to cover the first half. Using a tapestry needle, you now sew the section of 6 slst together to create the first leg opening. Fasten off and weave in the yarn end. Then, fold the second rectangle lengthwise in half and sew the 18 stitches of the rise and the 6 slst of the second leg opening together. Fasten off and weave in the yarn end.

WAISTBAND
(in subtle green)
Rejoin the subtle green yarn in a row-end at the back of the trousers.

Rnd 1: (sc in next 29 row-ends, dec) repeat 2 times [60]

Rnd 2 – 5: sc in all 60 st [60]

Rnd 6: slst in next 60 st [60]

Fasten off and weave in the yarn ends.

CARDIGAN

(in cream)
Ch 44. Crochet in rows.

Note: The ch 2 at the end of each row is a turning chain and does not count as a hdc stitch.

Row 1: start in third ch from the hook, hdc in next 42 st, ch 2, turn [42]

Row 2: hdc in next 6 st, hdc inc in next st, ch 9, skip next 7 st, hdc in next 14 st, ch 9, skip next 7 st, hdc inc in next st, hdc in next 6 st, ch 2, turn [48]

Row 3: hdc in next 48 st, ch 2, turn [48]

Row 4: (hdc in next 7 st, hdc inc in next st) repeat 6 times, ch 2, turn [54]

Row 5 – 6: hdc in next 54 st, ch 2, turn [54]

Row 7: (hdc in next 8 st, hdc inc in next st) repeat 6 times, ch 2, turn [60]

Row 8: hdc in next 60 sl, ch 1, turn [60]

Single crochet an edge all around the cardigan: sc in next 59 st on the waistband, 3 sc in last st, work about 12 sc up the first side, 3 sc in next stitch (corner of the neckline). Continue on the neckline, sc in next 41 st, 3 sc in last st, work about 12 sc down the other side, 3 sc in last st.

Fasten off and weave in the yarn ends.

SLEEVES
With the right side of the cardigan facing you, rejoin the cream yarn in the bottom right stitch of the armhole. Ch 2.

Rnd 1: hdc in next 9 st, 2 hdc in the side post of the armhole, hdc in next 7 st, 2 hdc in the side post of the armhole [20]

Rnd 2: hdc in all 20 st [20]

Rnd 3: (hdc in next st, hdc inc in next st) repeat 10 times [30]

Rnd 4 – 6: hdc in all 30 st [30]

Rnd 7: (hdc in next st, dec) repeat 10 times [20]

Rnd 8: hdc in all 20 st [20]

Rnd 9: ch 1, crab stitch in next 20 st [20]

Slst in next st. Fasten off and weave in the yarn ends.

BOBBLY EDGING OR POMPON BORDER
(with yellow fingering weight yarn and a size B-1 / 2 mm crochet hook)
Holding the cardigan upside down, with the front side facing you, join the yellow fingering weight yarn in the bottom right corner.

First pompon bobble: ch 5, 4-dc-bobble in third ch from the hook, ch 3, 4-dc-bobble in third ch from the hook. Join the two bobbles by making a slst in the third ch from the starting chain. Ch 2, slst in first st where the ch 5 starts. Do not fasten off but continue crocheting the next pompon bobbles.

Next pompon bobbles: (ch 5, 4-dc-bobble in third ch from the hook, ch 3, 4-dc-bobble in third ch from the hook. Join the two bobbles by making a slst in the third ch from the starting chain. Ch 2, skip 2 st, slst in next st) repeat until the end of the row [about 22 bobbles]

Fasten off and weave in the yarn ends.

Mabel Hedgehog

Mabel is a kindergarten teacher. You may see her dressing as a fairy (she's lucky to have Peggy Hippo as her friend) and singing and smiling all day long. And you might think: Oh! What an easy and fun job she has! And part of it is true, it's super fun, but it's not easy at all. Being a teacher to small critters is one of the most important jobs in the world: she has to help the little tots grasp the meaning of numbers and letters, but also has the hard task of teaching them social skills, such as taking turns, making conversation with peers, managing emotions. Mabel also is an excellent darts player. She started playing with her friend Angus a couple of years ago and quickly entered the league of professional dart players. Another excellent way to practice emotion management.

GALLERY: Scan or visit *www.amigurumi.com/4111* to share pictures and find inspiration.

Note: The head and body are worked in one piece.

CHEEKS

(make 2, in pastel pink)
Rnd 1: start 8 sc in a magic ring [8]
Slst in next st. Fasten off, leaving a long tail for sewing.

SNOUT

(in cream)
Rnd 1: start 5 sc in a magic ring [5]
Rnd 2: inc in all 5 st [10]
Rnd 3 – 5: sc in all 10 [10]
Rnd 6: (sc in next 4 st, inc in next st) repeat 2 times [12]
Fasten off, leaving a long tail for sewing. Embroider the nose and the mouth with black yarn.

HEAD AND BODY

(start in olive)
Rnd 1: start 6 sc in a magic ring [6]
Rnd 2: inc in all 6 st [12]
Rnd 3: (sc in next st, inc in next st) repeat 6 times [18]
Rnd 4: (sc in next 2 st, inc in next st) repeat 6 times [24]
Rnd 5: (sc in next 3 st, inc in next st) repeat 6 times [30]
Rnd 6: (sc in next 4 st, inc in next st) repeat 6 times [36]
Rnd 7: (sc in next 5 st, inc in next st) repeat 6 times [42]
Rnd 8: (sc in next 6 st, inc in next st) repeat 6 times [48]
Rnd 9: (sc in next 7 st, inc in next st) repeat 6 times [54]
Rnd 10: (sc in next 8 st, inc in next st) repeat 6 times [60]
Continue working with alternating yarns (olive and cream). The color you work with is indicated before each part.
Rnd 11: *(olive)* sc in next 21 st, *(cream)* sc in next 18 st, *(olive)* sc in next 21 st [60]
Rnd 12: *(olive)* sc in next 20 st, *(cream)* sc in next 20 st, *(olive)* sc in next 20 st [60]

Rnd 13: *(olive)* sc in next 19 st, *(cream)* sc in next 22 st, *(olive)* sc in next 19 st [60]

Rnd 14 – 20: *(olive)* sc in next 18 st, *(cream)* sc in next 24 st, *(olive)* sc in next 18 st [60]

Sew the snout between rounds 14 and 18 in the center of the cream patch. Stuff the snout lightly with fiberfill before closing the seam. Insert the safety eyes between rounds 16 and 17, about 3 stitches away from the snout. Sew the cheeks behind the safety eyes. Continue working in a jacquard pattern, alternating subtle green and teal green yarn according to the diagram.

Rnd 21 – 32: sc in all 60 st [60]

Continue working with alternating yarns (olive and cream). The color you work with is indicated before each part.

Note: In the next rounds, we're working the cream patch for the belly. If the cream belly patch doesn't line up nicely with the cream face patch, crochet a few more sc in olive yarn or undo them.

Rnd 33: work this round in BLO *(olive)* sc in next 24 st, *(cream)* sc in next 15 st, *(olive)* sc in next 21 st [60]

Rnd 34: *(olive)* sc in next 24 st, *(cream)* sc in next 15 st, *(olive)* sc in next 21 st [60]

Rnd 35: *(olive)* sc in next 25 st, *(cream)* sc in next 13 st, *(olive)* sc in next 22 st [60]

Continue working in olive yarn.

Rnd 36 – 37: sc in all 60 st [60]

Rnd 38: (sc in next 8 st, dec) repeat 6 times [54]

Rnd 39: (sc in next 7 st, dec) repeat 6 times [48]

Rnd 40: (sc in next 6 st, dec) repeat 6 times [42]

Rnd 41: sc in all 42 st [42]

Do not fasten off.

LEGS

To make the legs, divide the work identifying 6 stitches for the front central space between the legs, 6 stitches

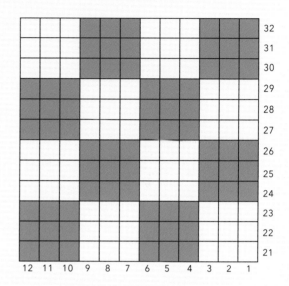

for the back and 15 stitches for each leg (you may find it useful to use stitch markers). If the legs don't line up nicely with the head, crochet a few more sc on the body or undo them. Join the first marked stitch for the leg on the back side to the marked stitch on the front side, working a single crochet stitch (this sc will be the first stitch of the leg). Now the stitches of the first leg are joined in the round. Continue working the first leg:

Rnd 42 – 43: sc in all 15 st [15]

Rnd 44: (sc in next 3 st, dec) repeat 3 times [12]

Rnd 45 – 47: sc in all 12 st [12]

Rnd 48: dec 6 times [6]

Fasten off, leaving a long tail. Using a tapestry needle, weave the yarn tail through the front loop of each remaining stitch and pull tight to close. Weave in the yarn end. Stuff the body and leg firmly.

SECOND LEG

Rejoin the olive yarn in the seventh unworked stitch at the back of round 41.

This is where we start the first stitch of the second leg. Leave a long starting yarn tail.

Rnd 42: sc in next 15 st. When you reach the 15th stitch of the leg, sc in first st to join the round [15]

Rnd 43 – 48: repeat the pattern for the first leg. Stuff the second leg and add more stuffing to the body if needed. Using a tapestry needle and the starting yarn tail, sew the 6 stitches between the legs closed.

ARMS

(make 2, in olive)

Rnd 1: start 6 sc in a magic ring [6]
Rnd 2: sc in all 6 st [6]
Rnd 3: (sc in next 2 st, inc in next st) repeat 2 times [8]
Rnd 4: sc in all 8 st [8]
Rnd 5: (sc in next 3 st, inc in next st) repeat 2 times [10]
Rnd 6 – 13: sc in all 10 st [10]
Fasten off, leaving a long tail for sewing. Stuff with fiberfill. Sew the arms to both sides between rounds 22 and 23.

EARS

(make 2, in cream)

Rnd 1: start 8 sc in a magic ring [8]
Rnd 2 – 4: sc in all 8 st [8]
Fasten off, leaving a long tail for sewing. Do not stuff. Flatten and sew the ears to the top of the head, over rounds 10 to 13, about 2 stitches away from the cream patch.

HAIR

(in olive)
Insert the hook in round 20 of the body, right next to the cream face patch. Pull up a loop of olive yarn.
Row 1: (ch 4, start in second ch from hook, slst in next 3 ch, slst in next st on the head) repeat in all olive stitches around the cream face patch. When you reach the bottom side of the cream face patch, turn your work and continue making hair strands in the other direction, repeating row 1 in all olive stitches of the head.

SKIRT

(start in mustard yellow)
Ch 56. Make sure your chain isn't twisted. Insert the hook in the first chain stitch and join the foundation chain with a slst. Continue working in a spiral.
Rnd 1: sc in all 56 st [56]
Rnd 2: (sc in next 6 st, inc in next st) repeat 8 times [64]
Rnd 3: sc in all 64 st [64]
Rnd 4: (sc in next 7 st, inc in next st) repeat 8 times [72]
Rnd 5: sc in all 72 st [72]

Rnd 6: (sc in next 8 st, inc in next st) repeat 8 times [80]
Rnd 7: sc in all 80 st [80]
Change to pale pink yarn.
Rnd 8: (sc in next st, skip next st, 5 dc in next st, skip next st) repeat 20 times [120]
Rnd 9: slst in all 120 st [120]
Fasten off and weave in the yarn ends.

WAISTBAND
(in mustard yellow)
Rejoin the mustard yellow yarn in the first stitch of round 1 of the skirt.
Rnd 1: sc in all 56 st [56]
Rnd 2: slst in all 56 st [56]
Fasten off and weave in the yarn ends.

FAIRY WINGS

BUTTON
(start in mustard yellow)
Rnd 1: start 6 sc in a magic ring [6]
Change to cream yarn.
Rnd 2: inc in all 6 st [12]
Continue in a stripe pattern, changing color every round, alternating mustard yellow and cream yarn.
Rnd 3: (sc in next st, inc in next st) repeat 6 times [18]
Rnd 4 – 5: sc in all 18 st [18]
Rnd 6: (sc in next st, dec) repeat 6 times [12]
Rnd 7: dec 6 times [6]
Fasten off, leaving a long tail for sewing. Do not stuff. Using a tapestry needle, weave the yarn tail through the front loop of each remaining stitch and pull tight to close.

WINGS

(make 2, in subtle green)

Rnd 1: start 5 sc in a magic ring [5]

Rnd 2: inc in all 5 st [10]

Rnd 3: (sc in next st, inc in next st) repeat 5 times [15]

Rnd 4: (sc in next 2 st, inc in next st) repeat 5 times [20]

Rnd 5 – 6: sc in all 20 st [20]

Rnd 7: (sc in next 8 st, dec) repeat 2 times [18]

Rnd 8 – 9: sc in all 18 st [18]

Rnd 10: (sc in next 7 st, dec) repeat 2 times [16]

Rnd 11 – 12: sc in all 16 st [16]

Rnd 13: (sc in next 6 st, dec) repeat 2 times [14]

Rnd 14 – 15: sc in all 14 st [14]

Rnd 16: (sc in next 5 st, dec) repeat 2 times [12]

Rnd 17 – 19: sc in all 12 st [12]

Rnd 20: dec 6 times [6]

Fasten off, leaving a long tail for sewing. The wings do not need to be stuffed. Use teal green yarn to embroider the embellishments on the wings. Flatten and sew them to the back of the button.

STRAPS

(in pale pink)

Ch 42. Make sure your chain isn't twisted. Insert the hook in the first chain stitch and join the foundation chain with a slst. Ch 42 again, and making sure your chain isn't twisted, insert the hook in the first chain to join the second foundation chain. You will have an 8-shape.

Rnd 1: slst in all 84 ch, all around the double foundation chain [84]

Fasten off. Sew the wings to the crossing center of the double foundation chain. Weave in the yarn ends.

Indiana Moth

Indiana has one of the coolest jobs around... she is an archivist! Ok, I know, it may not seem so attractive, and her species is not known for preserving things but, and probably because of that, she spent years studying and specializing in collecting, organizing, and maintaining valuable objects. And she's one of the best in her field. Indiana works shoulder to shoulder with Gertrude Dragon, the archaeologist. When Gertrude finds a very old manuscript, Indiana flies to the site and makes sure it is well preserved, so it never gets lost or damaged. They have become such close friends, that they are planning their summer holiday together. But they can't decide if they want an adventure or just a beach trip to relax.

GALLERY: Scan or visit www.amigurumi.com/4112 to share pictures and find inspiration.

Size:
14 inches / 36 cm tall when made with the indicated yarn (antennae included)

Materials:
– Worsted weight yarn in
  · cream
  · slate gray
  · pale pink
  · burnt orange
  · pastel pink
  · graphite gray
  · black (leftover)
– Size C-2 / 2.75 mm crochet hook
– Black oval safety eyes (12 mm)
– Tapestry needle
– Fiberfill

Skills needed: magic ring (page 32), work around a foundation chain (page 34), dividing the body in two parts (page 47), working jacquard crochet from a diagram (page 36), basket spike stitch (page 29), joining parts (page 39), embroidery (page 38)

Note: The head and body are worked in one piece.

CHEEKS

(make 2, in pastel pink)
Rnd 1: start 8 sc in a magic ring [8]
Slst in next st. Fasten off, leaving a long tail for sewing.

HEAD AND BODY

(start in cream)
Rnd 1: start 6 sc in a magic ring [6]
Rnd 2: inc in all 6 st [12]
Rnd 3: (sc in next st, inc in next st) repeat 6 times [18]
Rnd 4: (sc in next 2 st, inc in next st) repeat 6 times [24]
Rnd 5: (sc in next 3 st, inc in next st) repeat 6 times [30]
Rnd 6: (sc in next 4 st, inc in next st) repeat 6 times [36]
Rnd 7: (sc in next 5 st, inc in next st) repeat 6 times [42]

Rnd 8: (sc in next 6 st, inc in next st) repeat 6 times [48]
Rnd 9 – 14: sc in all 48 st [48]
Rnd 15: (sc in next 2 st, dec) repeat 12 times [36]
Rnd 16: (sc in next 4 st, dec) repeat 6 times [30]
Embroider the mouth with black yarn between rounds 12 and 13. The mouth must be embroidered on the opposite side of the start of the round. Insert the safety eyes between rounds 11 and 12, about 2 stitches away from the mouth. Sew the cheeks behind the safety eyes.
Rnd 17: inc in all 30 st [60]
Stuff the head and continue stuffing as you go. Change to slate gray yarn.

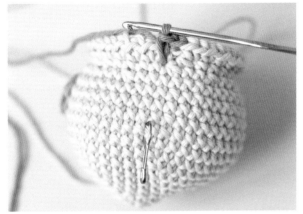

Rnd 18: (BLO sc in next st, spike st) repeat 30 times [60]
Change to cream yarn.
Rnd 19: (spike st, BLO sc in next st) repeat 30 times [60]
Continue in a stripe pattern, changing color every round, alternating slate gray and cream yarn.
Rnd 20 – 25: repeat rounds 18 and 19.
Change to pastel pink yarn.
Rnd 26: (sc in next st, dec) repeat 20 times [40]
Continue in jacquard pattern, alternating pastel pink, pale pink, burnt orange and slate gray yarn according to the diagram.
Rnd 27 – 42: sc in all 40 st [40]
Continue in a stripe pattern, changing color every round, alternating cream and slate gray yarn.
Rnd 43: (sc in next 8 st, dec) repeat 4 times [36]
Rnd 44: sc in all 36 st [36]
Rnd 45: (sc in next 4 st, dec) repeat 6 times [30]
Rnd 46: sc in all 30 st [30]
Rnd 47: (sc in next 3 st, dec) repeat 6 times [24]
Rnd 48: sc in all 24 st [24]
Rnd 49: (sc in next 2 st, dec) repeat 6 times [18]
Rnd 50: (sc in next st, dec) repeat 6 times [12]
Continue in slate gray yarn. Add more stuffing to the body if needed.
Rnd 51: dec 6 times [6]
Fasten off, leaving a long tail. Using a tapestry needle, weave the yarn tail through the front loop of each remaining stitch and pull tight to close. Weave in the yarn end.

ARMS

(make 2, in slate gray)
Rnd 1: start 7 sc in a magic ring [7]
Rnd 2 – 14: sc in all 7 st [7]
Fasten off, leaving a long tail for sewing. Stuff lightly with fiberfill. Sew the arms to both sides between rounds 26 and 27.

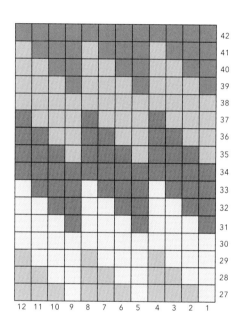

												42
												41
												40
												39
												38
												37
												36
												35
												34
												33
												32
												31
												30
												29
												28
												27
12	11	10	9	8	7	6	5	4	3	2	1	

LEGS

(make 2, in slate gray)
Rnd 1: start 7 sc in a magic ring [7]
Rnd 2 – 22: sc in all 7 st [7]
Fasten off, leaving a long tail for sewing. Stuff lightly with fiberfill. Sew the legs to both sides between rounds 41 and 42.

BOOTS

(make 2, in graphite gray)
Ch 6. Stitches are worked around both sides of the foundation chain.
Rnd 1: start in second ch from the hook, inc in this st, sc in next 3 st, 4 sc in last st. Continue on the other side of the foundation chain, sc in next 3 st, inc in

last st [14]

Rnd 2: inc in next 2 st, sc in next 4 st, inc in next 3 st, sc in next 4 st, inc in next st [20]

Rnd 3: BLO sc in next 9 st, dec 2 times, sc in next 7 st [18]

Rnd 4: sc in next 6 st, dec 4 times, sc in next 4 st [14]

Rnd 5: sc in next 6 st, dec 2 times, sc in next 4 st [12]

Rnd 6 – 7: sc in all 12 st [12]

Rnd 8: slst in all 12 st [12]

Fasten off and weave in the yarn end.

Join the graphite gray yarn in the last front loop stitch of round 3 and FLO slst in all 20 st. Fasten off and weave in the yarn end.

WINGS

(make 2, start in cream)

Leave a long starting yarn tail to sew the wing on later.

Rnd 1: start 6 sc in a magic ring [6]

Rnd 2: inc in all 6 st [12]

Rnd 3: sc in all 12 st [12]

Rnd 4: (sc in next 2 st, inc in next st) repeat 4 times [16]

Rnd 5: sc in all 16 st [16]

Rnd 6: (sc in next 3 st, inc in next st) repeat 4 times [20]

Rnd 7: sc in all 20 st [20]

Rnd 8: (sc in next 4 st, inc in next st) repeat 4 times [24]

Rnd 9: sc in all 24 st [24]

Rnd 10: (sc in next 5 st, inc in next st) repeat 4 times [28]

Rnd 11: sc in all 28 st [28]

Rnd 12: (sc in next 6 st, inc in next st) repeat 4 times [32]

Continue in a jacquard pattern, alternating cream, pastel pink and burnt orange yarn according to the diagram.

Rnd 13 – 20: sc in all 32 st [32]

Change to burnt orange yarn.

Rnd 21: sc in next 14 st, dec 2 times, sc in next 14 st [30]

Rnd 22: sc in all 30 st [30]

Rnd 23: sc in next 13 st, dec 2 times, sc in next 13 st [28]

Rnd 24: sc in all 28 st [28]

Rnd 25: sc in next 12 st, dec 2 times, sc in next 12 st [26]

Rnd 26: sc in all 26 st [26]

Rnd 27: sc in next 11 st, dec 2 times, sc in next 11 st [24]

Rnd 28: sc in all 24 st [24]

Rnd 29: (sc in next 4 st, dec) repeat 4 times [20]

Rnd 30: (sc in next 3 st, dec) repeat 4 times [16]

Rnd 31: (sc in next 2 st, dec) repeat 4 times [12]

Rnd 32: dec 6 times [6]

Fasten off, leaving a long tail. Do not stuff. Using the tapestry needle, weave the yarn tail through the front loop of each remaining stitch and pull tight to close. Weave in the yarn end. Sew the wings to the back between rounds 20 and 24. With pastel pink yarn, make a 2" / 5 cm pompon and sew it to the back, over rounds 20 and 22, between the wings.

ANTENNAE

(make 2, in slate gray)

Rnd 1: start 6 sc in a magic ring [6]

Rnd 2: sc in all 6 st [6]

Rnd 3: (sc in next st, inc in next st) repeat 3 times [9]

Rnd 4 – 5: sc in all 9 st [9]

Rnd 6: (sc in next 2 st, inc in next st) repeat 3 times [12]

Rnd 7 – 8: sc in all 12 st [12]

Rnd 9: (sc in next 3 st, inc in next st) repeat 3 times [15]

Rnd 10 – 13: sc in all 15 st [15]

Rnd 14: (sc in next st, dec) repeat 5 times [10]

Rnd 15: sc in all 10 st [10]

Rnd 16: (sc in next 3 st, dec) repeat 2 times [8]

Fasten off, leaving a long tail for sewing. Do not stuff. Embroider the embellishments on the antennae with cream yarn. Flatten them before sewing them on top of the head.

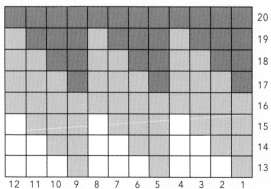

Alberto Seagull

Everyone loves Alberto. While we all agree that seagulls aren't the most perfect birds in the animal kingdom — a bit too noisy, not always in the best mood and with a controversial diet (they love eating trash) — everyone thinks Alberto is perfect in his own way. He is a professional photographer. He's the best at aerial photography and his work has been exhibited in the most exclusive galleries in the world as well as museums. Alberto was also a lover of crab patties, but that changed when he met Philip Lobster. From that moment on he eliminated all crustaceans from his diet and is trying to change to plant-based meals only... at least when Philip is around.

GALLERY: Scan or visit *www.amigurumi.com/4113* to share pictures and find inspiration.

Size:
11 inches / 28 cm tall when made with the indicated yarn

Materials:
– Worsted weight yarn in
 · off-white
 · yellow
 · white
 · French blue
 · ash gray
 · graphite gray (leftover)
 · pastel pink
 · subtle green
– Size C-2 / 2.75 mm crochet hook
– Size D-3 / 3.25 mm crochet hook (optional)
– Black safety eyes (8 mm)
– Tapestry needle
– Fiberfill

Skills needed: magic ring *(page 32)*, crochet an elongated back *(explained in the pattern)*, embroidery *(page 38)*, joining parts *(page 39)*

Note: The head and body are worked in one piece.

Note: Use a size C-2 / 2.75 mm crochet hook, unless otherwise noted.

BEAK

(in yellow)
Rnd 1: start 6 sc in a magic ring [6]
Rnd 2: inc in all 6 st [12]
Rnd 3 – 12: sc in all 12 st [12]
Fasten off, leaving a long tail for sewing. Stuff lightly.

HEAD AND BODY

(start in off-white)
Rnd 1: start 6 sc in a magic ring [6]
Rnd 2: inc in all 6 st [12]
Rnd 3: (sc in next st, inc in next st) repeat 6 times [18]
Rnd 4: (sc in next 2 st, inc in next st) repeat 6 times [24]

Rnd 5: (sc in next 3 st, inc in next st) repeat 6 times [30]
Rnd 6: (sc in next 4 st, inc in next st) repeat 6 times [36]
Rnd 7 – 19: sc in all 36 st [36]
Change to French blue yarn.
Rnd 20: sc in all 36 st [36]
Sew the beak between rounds 15 and 19. Insert the safety eyes between rounds 15 and 16, about 3 stitches away from the beak. Embroider the cheeks with pastel pink yarn.
Continue in a stripe pattern, alternating 2 rounds in white and 1 round in French blue yarn.
Rnd 21 – 35: sc in all 36 st [36]
Change to off-white yarn.
Rnd 36: BLO sc in all 36 st [36]
Rnd 37: Find the middle back of the seagull body. If you are not there yet, continue crocheting until that point. Then, ch 9. (Place a stitch marker in the next st you make – the first you will make on the foundation chain, this will mark the beginning of the next rounds.) Crochet back on the chain, start in second ch from the hook, sc in next

125

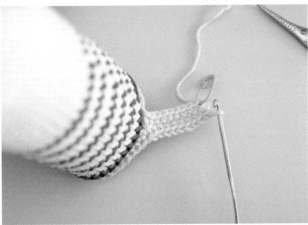

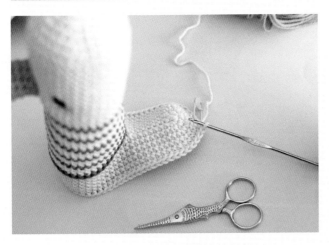

8 st, sc in the stitch where the foundation chain starts, continue on the body and sc in next 36 st, continue on the other side of the chain and sc in next 7 st, inc in last st [54]

Rnd 38: inc in next 2 st, sc in next 50 st, inc in next 2 st [58]

Rnd 39: inc in next 3 st, sc in next 53 st, inc in next 2 st [63]

Rnd 40 – 42: sc in all 63 st [63]

Stuff the body and continue stuffing as you go.

Rnd 43: sc in next 4 st, dec, sc in next 52 st, dec, sc in next 3 st [61]

Rnd 44: sc in all 61 st [61]

Rnd 45: sc in next 4 st, dec, sc in next 50 st, dec, sc in next 3 st [59]

Rnd 46: sc in all 59 st [59]

Rnd 47: sc in next 4 st, dec, sc in next 48 st, dec, sc in next 3 st [57]

Rnd 48: sc in next 24 st, dec, sc in next 6 st, dec, sc in next 23 st [55]

Rnd 49: sc in next 4 st, dec, sc in next 44 st, dec, sc in next 3 st [53]

Rnd 50: sc in next 22 st, dec, sc in next 6 st, dec, sc in next 21 st [51]

Rnd 51: sc in next 4 st, dec, sc in next 19 st, dec, sc in next 19 st, dec, sc in next 3 st [48]

Rnd 52: (sc in next 6 st, dec) repeat 6 times [42]

Rnd 53: (sc in next 5 st, dec) repeat 6 times [36]

Rnd 54: (sc in next 4 st, dec) repeat 6 times [30]

Rnd 55: (sc in next 3 st, dec) repeat 6 times [24]

Rnd 56: (sc in next 2 st, dec) repeat 6 times [18]

Rnd 57: (sc in next st, dec) repeat 6 times [12]

Rnd 58: dec 6 times [6]

Fasten off, leaving a long tail. Add more stuffing if needed. Using a tapestry needle, weave the yarn tail through the front loop of each remaining stitch and pull tight to close. Weave in the yarn end.

LEGS

(make 2, in yellow)
Leave a long starting yarn tail. Ch 10. Make sure your chain isn't twisted. Insert the hook in the first chain stitch and join the foundation chain with a slst. Continue working in a spiral.
Rnd 1 – 10: sc in all 10 st [10]
Fasten off, leaving a long tail for sewing. Stuff the leg.
Note: Make sure to stuff the legs with enough fiberfill, without overstuffing, so that the seagull holds up as well as possible (but always remember that he's a crocheted toy made with yarn, so do not get frustrated if he cannot stand all by himself).

Fasten off, leaving a long tail for sewing. Do not stuff. Flatten and, using a tapestry needle, close the opening of the last round. Sew the feet to the legs. Sew the legs to the body between rounds 52 to 55.

FEET

(make 2, in yellow)
Rnd 1: start 5 sc in a magic ring [5]
Rnd 2: sc in all 5 st [5]
Rnd 3: inc in all 5 st [10]
Rnd 4: sc in all 10 st [10]
Rnd 5: (sc in next st, inc in next st) repeat 5 times [15]
Rnd 6: sc in all 15 st [15]
Rnd 7: (sc in next 2 st, inc in next st) repeat 5 times [20]
Rnd 8: sc in all 20 st [20]
Rnd 9: (sc in next 3 st, inc in next st) repeat 5 times [25]
Rnd 10 – 11: sc in all 25 st [25]

WINGS

(make 2, in ash gray)
Rnd 1: start 6 sc in a magic ring [6]
Rnd 2: inc in all 6 st [12]
Rnd 3: (sc in next st, inc in next st) repeat 6 times [18]
Rnd 4: (sc in next 2 st, inc in next st) repeat 6 times [24]
Rnd 5: (sc in next 3 st, inc in next st) repeat 6 times [30]
Rnd 6 – 8: sc in all 30 st [30]
Fasten off, leaving a long tail for sewing. The wings do not need to be stuffed. Flatten and sew the wings to both sides of the body between rounds 41 and 42.

TAIL

(in graphite gray)
Rnd 1: start 8 sc in a magic ring [8]
Rnd 2 – 8: sc in all 8 st [8]
Fasten off, leaving a long tail for sewing.
The tail does not need to be stuffed.
Flatten the tail. Sew the tail to the back,
centered over rounds 39 and 40.

HAT

**(in pastel pink, using a size D-3 / 3.25 mm
crochet hook)**
Note: You can work the hat with the same
crochet hook size that you used for the
rest of the body, but just keep in mind that
the result might be tighter, so you'll have
to add a few more rows or loosen your
tension a bit.
Ch 20. Crochet in rows.
Row 1: start in third ch from the hook,
hdc in next 18 st, ch 2, turn [18]
Row 2 – 18: BLO hdc in all 18 st, ch 2,
turn [18]
Fasten off, leaving a long tail for sewing.

You will end with a crochet rectangle. Line
up row 1 and 18 and, using a tapestry
needle, sew both sides together to form
a tube. Do not fasten off. Using the same
yarn tail, sew through each row-end at
the top of the tube. Pull the yarn tail so
the round tightens and weave in the ends
by sewing back and forth to close the hat
opening. Flip the hat inside out.

With subtle green yarn, make a 1.2 inches /
3 cm pompon and sew it to the top of the
hat.

Astrid Ostrich

Astrid was the most curious but also the most introverted and shy tiny big bird. She spent most of her childhood watching adventure films. From Indiana Jones to The Goonies, from 20.000 leagues under the sea to The Adventures of Robin Hood, superheroes movies and sci-fi, even romantic movies. Astrid learned the lines by heart, she even studied the composition and camera angles. When she was tall enough to hold a camera, she started filming her own short movies. Probably none of those films will go down in history as classics, but Astrid plans to start Film School, so her oeuvre will definitely improve. Recently, she discovered French cinema and now she doesn't set foot outside without her beret. As cliche as it may look, it does make her happy. And that's all that matters.

SKILL LEVEL *

Size:
16 inches / 40 cm tall when made with the indicated yarn

Materials:
– Worsted weight yarn in
  · pastel mint
  · teal green
  · greenish gray (leftover)
  · French blue
  · pastel pink
  · off-white
  · yellow
– Size C-2 / 2.75 mm crochet hook
– Black safety eyes (10 mm)
– Tapestry needle
– Fiberfill

Skills needed: magic ring *(page 32)*, changing color at the beginning of a round *(page 35)*, changing color mid-round *(page 35)*, work around a foundation chain *(page 34)*, crochet an elongated back *(page 126)*, embroidery *(page 38)*, joining parts *(page 39)*

Note: The head and body are worked in one piece.

CHEEKS

(make 2, in greenish gray)
Rnd 1: start 6 sc in a magic ring [6]
Rnd 2: inc in all 6 st [12]
Slst in next st. Fasten off, leaving a long tail for sewing.

BEAK

(in pastel pink)
Rnd 1: start 6 sc in a magic ring [6]
Rnd 2: inc in all 6 st [12]
Rnd 3 – 4: sc in all 12 st [12]
Rnd 5: (sc in next 5 st, inc in next st) repeat 2 times [14]
Rnd 6 – 7: sc in all 14 st [14]
Rnd 8: (sc in next 6 st, inc in next st) repeat 2 times [16]
Rnd 9 – 10: sc in all 16 st [16]
Rnd 11: (sc in next 7 st, inc in next st) repeat 2 times [18]
Rnd 12 – 13: sc in all 18 st [18]
Rnd 14: (sc in next 8 st, inc in next st) repeat 2 times [20]
Rnd 15: sc in all 20 st [20]
Fasten off, leaving a long tail for sewing. Stuff lightly with fiberfill.

HEAD AND BODY

(start in pastel mint)
Rnd 1: start 6 sc in a magic ring [6]
Rnd 2: inc in all 6 st [12]
Rnd 3: (sc in next st, inc in next st) repeat 6 times [18]
Rnd 4: (sc in next st, inc in next st) repeat 9 times [27]
Rnd 5: (sc in next 2 st, inc in next st) repeat 9 times [36]
Rnd 6: (sc in next 3 st, inc in next st) repeat 9 times [45]
Rnd 7: (sc in next 4 st, inc in next st) repeat 9 times [54]
Rnd 8 – 10: sc in all 54 st [54]
Rnd 11: (sc in next 8 st, inc in next st) repeat 6 times [60]
Rnd 12 – 14: sc in all 60 st [60]
Rnd 15: (sc in next 9 st, inc in next st) repeat 6 times [66]
Rnd 16 – 19: sc in all 66 st [66]
Rnd 20: (sc in next 9 st, dec) repeat 6 times [60]
Rnd 21: (sc in next 3 st, dec) repeat 12 times [48]

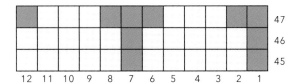

												47
												46
												45

12 11 10 9 8 7 6 5 4 3 2 1

Rnd 22: (sc in next 2 st, dec) repeat 12 times [36]

Sew the beak between rounds 13 and 17. The beak must be placed on the opposite side of the start of the round. Insert the safety eyes between rounds 15 and 16, about 2 stitches away from the beak. Sew the cheeks between rounds 14 and 18.

Rnd 23: (sc in next 4 st, dec) repeat 6 times [30]

Rnd 24: (sc in next 3 st, dec) repeat 6 times [24]

Stuff the head and continue stuffing the body as you go.

Rnd 25 – 44: sc in all 24 st [24]

Continue in a jacquard pattern, alternating pastel mint and teal green yarn according to the diagram.

Note: In round 45 the increase counts as 2 stitches. This means that sometimes the increase will be made with 2 stitches of the same color, and sometimes it will be made with one stitch in each color.

Rnd 45: (sc in next 3 st, inc in next st) repeat 6 times [30]

Rnd 46 – 47: sc in all 30 st [30]

Continue in teal green yarn.

Rnd 48: (sc in next 4 st, inc in next st) repeat 6 times [36]

Rnd 49: sc in all 36 st [36]

Rnd 50: (sc in next 2 st, inc in next st) repeat 12 times [48]

Rnd 51: sc in all 48 st [48]

Rnd 52: (sc in next 3 st, inc in next st) repeat 12 times [60]

Rnd 53: sc in all 60 st [60]

Rnd 54: Find the middle back of the ostrich body. If you are not there yet, continue crocheting until that point (I had to crochet 9 sc to get there). Then, ch 6. (Place a stitch marker in the next st you make – the first you will make on the foundation chain, this will mark the beginning of the next rounds.) Crochet back on the chain, inc in second ch from hook, sc in next 4 st, sc in the stitch where the foundation chain starts, continue on the body and sc in next 60 st, continue on the other side of the chain and sc in next 4 st, inc in last st [73]

Rnd 55: inc in next 2 st, sc in next 69 st, inc in next 2 st [77]

Rnd 56: inc in next 3 st, sc in next 72 st, inc in next 2 st [82]

Rnd 57 – 59: sc in all 82 st [82]

Rnd 60: sc in next 5 st, dec, sc in next 70 st, dec, sc in next 3 st [80]

Rnd 61: sc in all 80 st [80]

Rnd 62: sc in next 5 st, dec, sc in next 68 st, dec, sc in next 3 st [78]

Rnd 63: sc in all 78 st [78]

Rnd 64: sc in next 5 st, dec, sc in next 26 st, dec, sc in next 8 st, dec, sc in next 28 st, dec, sc in next 3 st [74]

Rnd 65: sc in all 74 st [74]

Rnd 66: sc in next 5 st, dec, sc in next 24 st, dec, sc in next 8 st, dec, sc in next 26 st, dec, sc in next 3 st [70]

Rnd 67: sc in all 70 st [70]

Rnd 68: (sc in next 5 st, dec) repeat 10 times [60]

Rnd 69: (sc in next 8 st, dec) repeat 6 times [54]

Rnd 70: (sc in next 7 st, dec) repeat 6 times [48]

Rnd 71: (sc in next 6 st, dec) repeat 6 times [42]

Rnd 72: (sc in next 5 st, dec) repeat 6 times [36]

Rnd 73: (sc in next 4 st, dec) repeat 6 times [30]

Rnd 74: (sc in next 3 st, dec) repeat 6 times [24]

Rnd 75: (sc in next 2 st, dec) repeat 6 times [18]

Rnd 76: (sc in next st, dec) repeat 6 times [12]

Rnd 77: dec 6 times [6]

Fasten off, leaving a long tail. Using a tapestry needle, weave the yarn tail through the front loop of each remaining stitch and pull tight to close. Weave in the yarn end.

LEGS

(make 2, start in teal green)
Leave a long starting yarn tail and ch 14. Make sure your chain isn't twisted. Insert the hook in the first chain stitch and join the foundation chain with a slst. Continue working in a spiral. Work in a stripe pattern, changing color every round, alternating teal green and off-white yarn.
Rnd 1 – 8: sc in all 14 st [14]
Continue in pastel pink yarn. Stuff with fiberfill and continue stuffing as you go.
Rnd 9 – 24: sc in all 14 st [14]
Fasten off, leaving a long tail for sewing.

FEET

(make 2, in pastel pink)
Start with the toes, make 3.
Rnd 1: start 8 sc in a magic ring [8]
Rnd 2 – 6: sc in all 8 st [8]
Fasten off the first and second toe, leaving a yarn tail. Do not fasten off the third toe. We will be joining the toes to make the foot.
Rnd 7: sc in next 4 st on the second toe, sc in all 8 st on the first toe, sc in leftover 4 st on the second toe, sc in all 8 st on the third toe [24]
You can sew the gaps between the toes closed using your tapestry needle and the

leftover yarn tails. Stuff the toes a little.
Rnd 8 – 10: sc in all 24 st [24]
Rnd 11: (sc in next 4 st, dec) repeat 4 times [20]
Rnd 12: sc in all 20 st [20]
Rnd 13: (sc in next 3 st, dec) repeat 4 times [16]
Rnd 14: sc in all 16 st [16]
Rnd 15: (sc in next 2 st, dec) repeat 4 times [12]
Rnd 16: sc in all 12 st [12]
Rnd 17: (sc in next 2 st, dec) repeat 3 times [9]
Stuff the feet a little more.
Rnd 18: (sc in next st, dec) repeat 3 times [6]
Fasten off, leaving a long tail. Using a tapestry needle, weave the yarn tail through the front loop of each remaining stitch and pull tight to close. Weave in the yarn end. Sew the feet to the legs.

WINGS

(make 2, start in teal green)
Leave a long starting yarn tail to sew the wings to the body.
Rnd 1: start 6 sc in a magic ring [6]
Rnd 2: inc in all 6 st [12]
Rnd 3: (sc in next st, inc in next st) repeat 6 times [18]
Rnd 4: (sc in next 2 st, inc in next st) repeat 6 times [24]
Rnd 5: (sc in next 3 st, inc in next st) repeat 6 times [30]
Rnd 6: (sc in next 4 st, inc in next st) repeat 6 times [36]
Rnd 7 – 12: sc in all 36 st [36]
Change to pastel mint yarn. Do not stuff. Next, we will divide the wing to make 3 feathers, using 12 stitches for each feather.

FIRST FEATHER
Rnd 1: skip 24 st and join the last stitch to the 25th stitch of the previous round with a sc stitch, sc in next 11 st [12]
Rnd 2 – 12: sc in all 12 st [12]
Rnd 13: dec 6 times [6]

Fasten off, leaving a long tail. Using a tapestry needle, weave the yarn tail through the front loop of each remaining stitch and pull tight to close. Weave in the yarn end.

SECOND FEATHER
Rejoin the pastel mint yarn to the stitch to the left of the first feather.
Rnd 1: sc in next 6 st and join the last stitch to the 6th stitch to the right side of the first feather. This sc will be the first stitch of the next round.
Rnd 2 – 13: repeat the pattern for the first feather.
Fasten off, leaving a long tail. Using a tapestry needle, weave the yarn tail through the front loop of each remaining stitch and pull tight to close. Weave in the yarn end.

THIRD FEATHER
Rejoin the pastel mint yarn to the stitch to the left of the second feather.
Rnd 1: sc in all 12 st [12]
Rnd 2 – 13: repeat the pattern for the first feather.
Fasten off, leaving a long tail. Using a tapestry needle, weave the yarn tail through the front loop of each remaining stitch and pull tight to close. Weave in the yarn end.
Use yellow yarn to embroider the embellishments on the feathers. Sew the wings over rounds 52 to 65. You can put some fiberfill stuffing between the wings and the body of the ostrich.

TAIL

LARGE FEATHER
(in pastel mint)
Rnd 1: start 5 sc in a magic ring [5]
Rnd 2: inc in all 5 st [10]
Rnd 3: (sc in next st, inc in next st) repeat 5 times [15]
Rnd 4: (sc in next 2 st, inc in next st) repeat 5 times [20]
Rnd 5 – 6: sc in all 20 st [20]
Rnd 7: (sc in next 8 st, dec) repeat 2 times [18]
Rnd 8 – 9: sc in all 18 st [18]
Rnd 10: (sc in next 7 st, dec) repeat 2 times [16]
Rnd 11 – 12: sc in all 16 st [16]
Rnd 13: (sc in next 6 st, dec) repeat 2 times [14]
Rnd 14 – 15: sc in all 14 st [14]

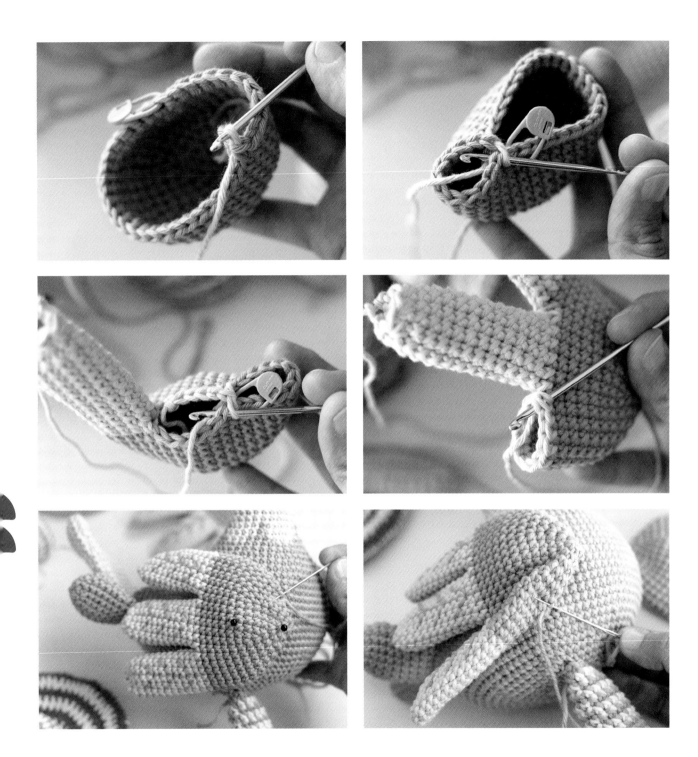

Rnd 16: (sc in next 5 st, dec) repeat 2 times [12]
Rnd 17: sc in all 12 st [12]
Fasten off, leaving long tail for sewing. The large feather does not need to be stuffed. Use yellow yarn to embroider the embellishments. Flatten and sew the large feather to the back, centered over rounds 55 and 56.

SMALL FEATHER
(make 2, in teal green)
Rnd 1: start 6 sc in a magic ring [6]
Rnd 2: inc in all 6 st [12]
Rnd 3: (sc in next 2 st, inc in next st) repeat 4 times [16]
Rnd 4 – 5: sc in all 16 st [16]
Rnd 6: (sc in next 6 st, dec) repeat 2 times [14]
Rnd 7 – 8: sc in all 14 st [14]
Rnd 9: (sc in next 5 st, dec) repeat 2 times [12]
Rnd 10: sc in all 12 st [12]
Fasten off, leaving a long tail for sewing. The small feathers do not need to be stuffed. Flatten and sew the small feathers below the large feather, one next to the other, between rounds 57 and 58.

BERET

(start in off-white)
Work in a stripe pattern, changing color every round, alternating off-white and blue yarn. Work in joined rounds.
Note: If you make the beret in a single color, there is no need to join the rounds.
Rnd 1: start 9 hdc in a magic ring, slst in first st, ch 1 [9]
Rnd 2: hdc inc in all 9 st, slst in first st, ch 1 [18]
Rnd 3: (hdc in next st, hdc inc in next st) repeat 9 times, slst in first st to join the round, ch 1 [27]
Rnd 4: (hdc in next 2 st, hdc inc in next st) repeat 9 times, slst in first st to join the round, ch 1 [36]
Rnd 5: (hdc in next 3 st, hdc inc in next st) repeat 9 times, slst in first st to join the round, ch 1 [45]
Rnd 6: (hdc in next 4 st, hdc inc in next st) repeat 9 times, slst in first st to join the round, ch 1 [54]
Rnd 7: (hdc in next 2 st, hdc inc in next st) repeat

18 times, slst in first st to join the round, ch 1 [72]
Rnd 8: (hdc in next 3 st, hdc inc in next st) repeat 18 times, slst in first st to join the round, ch 1 [90]
Rnd 9: hdc in all 90 st, slst in first st to join the round, ch 1 [90]
Rnd 10: (hdc in next 3 st, hdc dec) repeat 18 times, slst in first st to join the round, ch 1 [72]
Rnd 11: (hdc in next 2 st, hdc dec) repeat 18 times, slst in first st to join the round, ch 1 [54]
Change to pastel pink yarn.
Rnd 12 – 13: sc in all 54 st, slst in first st to join the round, ch 1 [54]
Rnd 14: slst in al 54 st, slst in first st to join the round [54]
Fasten off and weave in the yarn ends.

RIBBON
(start in pastel pink)
Ch 19. Crochet in rows
Row 1: start in second ch from hook, slst in all 18 st, ch 1, turn [18]
Change to off-white yarn.
Row 2 – 3: BLO slst in all 18 st, ch 1, turn [18]
Change to pink yarn.
Row 4: BLO slst in all 18 st, ch 1, turn [18]
Row 5: BLO slst in all 18 st [18]
Fasten off, leaving a long tail for sewing. Sew the ribbon on the inside of the beret, row 12

POMPON
(start in yellow)
Rnd 1: start 6 sc in a magic ring [6]
Continue in a stripe pattern, changing color every round, alternating off-white and yellow yarn.
Rnd 2: inc in all 6 st [12]
Rnd 3: (sc in next st, inc in next st) repeat 6 times [18]
Rnd 4: (sc in next 2 st, inc in next st) repeat 6 times [24]
Rnd 5 – 8: sc in all 24 st [24]
Rnd 9: (sc in next 2 st, dec) repeat 6 times [18]
Rnd 10: (sc in next st, dec) repeat 6 times [12]
Stuff the pompon with fiberfill.
Rnd 11: dec 6 times [6]
Fasten off, leaving a long tail for sewing. Sew the pompon to the top of the beret.

Greta Hen

As all members of her family, Greta learned crochet, knitting and embroidery when she was only a little chick. And then she got bored of all that. She felt it was a pastime for old hens. And she was anything but an old hen. Years passed. Greta pursued an art career but couldn't find her place in the world. Until one day she saw an art installation made from yarn. All the skills she was taught in one gigantic piece of art that blew her away. Now, Greta happily confirms the crafter stereotype: she loves period drama, her cup of tea, chatting with her friends and, of course, stocking the biggest yarn stash you could possibly imagine. Since she's a yarn artist, she has a reasonable excuse. But it IS a lot of yarn. A don't-tell-your-friends-because-they-probably-think-you're-insane lot of yarn.

GALLERY: Scan or visit *www.amigurumi.com/4115* to share pictures and find inspiration.

SKILL LEVEL * *

Size:
12.5 inches / 32 cm tall when made with the indicated yarn (comb included)

Materials:
– Worsted weight yarn in
· cream
· yellow
· brick red
· pastel pink (leftover)
· pastel mint
· graphite gray
– Size C-2 / 2.75 mm crochet hook
– Size D-3 / 3.25 mm crochet hook
– Black safety eyes (8 mm)
– Tapestry needle
– Fiberfill

Skills needed: magic ring *(page 32)*, dividing the body in two parts *(page 47)*, working around a foundation chain *(page 34)*, crochet an elongated back *(page 126)*, embroidery *(page 38)*, joining parts *(page 39)*

Note: *Use a size C-2 / 2.75 mm crochet hook, unless otherwise noted.*

Note: *The head and body are worked in one piece.*

CHEEKS

(make 2, in pastel pink)
Rnd 1: start 6 sc in a magic ring [6]
Rnd 2: inc in all 6 st [12]
Fasten off, leaving a long tail for sewing.

BEAK

(in yellow)
Rnd 1: start 5 sc in a magic ring [5]
Rnd 2: sc in all 5 st [5]
Rnd 3: (sc in next st, inc in next st) repeat 2 times, sc in next st [7]
Rnd 4: sc in all 7 st [7]
Rnd 5: (sc in next 2 st, inc in next st) repeat 2 times, sc in next st [9]
Rnd 6 – 7: sc in all 9 st [9]
Fasten off, leaving a long tail for sewing. Stuff lightly.

HEAD AND BODY

(in cream)
Rnd 1: start 6 sc in a magic ring [6]
Rnd 2: inc in all 6 st [12]
Rnd 3: (sc in next st, inc in next st) repeat 6 times [18]
Rnd 4: (sc in next 2 st, inc in next st) repeat 6 times [24]
Rnd 5: (sc in next 3 st, inc in next st) repeat 6 times [30]
Rnd 6: (sc in next 4 st, inc in next st) repeat 6 times [36]
Rnd 7: (sc in next 5 st, inc in next st) repeat 6 times [42]
Rnd 8 – 21: sc in all 42 st [42]
Sew the beak between rounds 11 and 14. The beak must be placed on the opposite side of the start of the round. Insert the safety eyes between rounds 12 and 13, about 3 stitches away from the beak. Sew the cheeks below the safety eyes.
Rnd 22: sc in next 10 st, inc in next st, sc in next 20 st, inc in next st, sc in next 10 st [44]
Rnd 23 – 25: sc in all 44 st [44]
Rnd 26: (sc in next 10 st, inc in next st)

repeat 4 times [48]

Rnd 27 – 29: sc in all 48 st [48]

Rnd 30: Find the middle back of the hen body. If you are not there yet, continue crocheting until that point. Then, ch 13. (Place a stitch marker in the next st you make – the first you will make on the foundation chain, this will mark the beginning of the next rounds.) Crochet back on the chain, inc in second ch from the hook, sc in next 11 st, sc in the stitch where the foundation chain starts, continue on the body and sc in next 21 st, inc in next st, sc in next 4 st, inc in next st, sc in next 21 st, continue on the other side of the chain and sc in next 11 st, inc in last st [77]

Rnd 31: inc next 2 st, sc in next 73 st, inc in next 2 st [81]

Rnd 32: inc in next 3 st, sc in next 35 st, inc in next st, sc in next 5 st, inc in next st, sc in next 34 st, inc in next 2 st [88]

Rnd 33: sc in all 88 st [88]

Rnd 34: sc in next st, inc in next st, sc in next 2 st, inc in next st, sc in next 36 st, (inc in next st, sc in next 3 st) repeat 2 times, inc in next st, sc in next 36 st, inc in next st, sc in next st [94]

Rnd 35 – 36: sc in all 94 st [94]

Rnd 37: sc in next 5 st, dec, sc in next 37 st, inc in next st, sc in next 9 st, inc in next st, sc in next 35 st, dec, sc in next 2 st [94]

Rnd 38: sc in all 94 st [94]

Rnd 39: sc in next 5 st, dec, sc in next 83 st, dec, sc in next 2 st [92]

Rnd 40: sc in all 92 st [92]

Rnd 41: sc in next 5 st, dec, sc in next 81 st, dec, sc in next 2 st [90]

Rnd 42 – 43: sc in all 90 st [90]

Rnd 44: sc in next 5 st, dec, sc in next 34 st, dec, sc in next 9 st, dec, sc in next 32 st, dec, sc in next 2 st [86]

Rnd 45 – 46: sc in all 86 st [86]

Rnd 47: sc in next 5 st, dec, sc in next 32 st, dec, sc in next 9 st, dec, sc in next 30 st, dec, sc in next 2 st [82]

Rnd 48: sc in all 82 st [82]

Rnd 49: sc in next 5 st, dec, sc in next 31 st, dec, sc in next 8 st, dec, sc in next 28 st, dec, sc in next 2 st [78]

Rnd 50: sc in all 78 st [78]

Rnd 51: (sc in next 11 st, dec) repeat 6 times [72]

Rnd 52: sc in all 72 st [72]

Rnd 53: (sc in next 10 st, dec) repeat 6 times [66]

Rnd 54: (sc in next 9 st, dec) repeat 6 times [60]

Rnd 55: (sc in next 8 st, dec) repeat 6 times [54]

Rnd 56: (sc in next 7 st, dec) repeat 6 times [48]

Stuff the head and neck. Do not fasten off.

LEGS

To make the legs, divide the work identifying 24 stitches for each leg. Find the middle back stitch. If you are not there yet, continue crocheting until that point or undo some stitches if needed. Ch 8 and join the last chain stitch to the 24th stitch of the previous round, working a single crochet stitch (this sc will be the first stitch of the leg). Now the stitches of the first leg are joined in the round. Continue working the first leg:

Rnd 57: sc in next 24 st on the body, BLO sc in next 8 ch [32]
Rnd 58 – 59: sc in all 32 st [32]
Rnd 60: (sc in next 2 st, dec) repeat 8 times [24]
Rnd 61: sc in all 24 st [24]
Rnd 62: (sc in next st, dec) repeat 8 times [16]
Change to yellow yarn.
Rnd 63: BLO (sc in next 2 st, dec) repeat 4 times [12]
Rnd 64 – 69: sc in all 12 st [12]
Fasten off, leaving a long tail for sewing. Stuff the body and the leg firmly.

SECOND LEG
Rejoin the cream yarn in the first unworked stitch at the back of round 56. This is where we start the first stitch of the second leg.
Rnd 57: sc in next 24 on the body, FLO sc in next 8 ch, sc in first st to join the round [32]
Rnd 58 – 69: repeat the pattern for the first leg.
Fasten off, leaving a long tail for sewing. Stuff the leg firmly.

FEET
(make 2, in yellow)
Start with the toes, make 3.
Rnd 1: start 8 sc in a magic ring [8]
Rnd 2 – 6: sc in all 8 st [8]
Fasten off the first and second toe, leaving a tail for sewing. Don't fasten off the third toe. We will be joining the toes to make the foot.
Rnd 7: sc in next 4 st on the second toe, sc in all 8 st on the first toe, sc in leftover 4 st on the second toe, sc in all 8 st on the third toe [24]
You can sew the holes between the toes closed using your tapestry needle and the leftover yarn tails. Stuff them lightly.
Rnd 8: sc in all 24 st [24]
Rnd 9: (sc in next 4 st, dec) repeat 4 times [20]
Rnd 10: sc in all 20 st [20]
Rnd 11: (sc in next 3 st, dec) repeat 4 times [16]
Rnd 12 – 13: sc in all 16 st [16]
Rnd 14: (sc in next 2 st, dec) repeat 4 times [12]
Stuff the feet lightly.
Rnd 15: (sc in next st, dec) repeat 4 times [8]

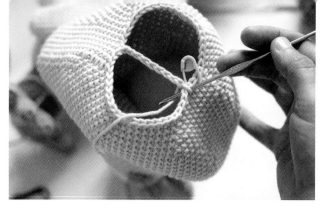

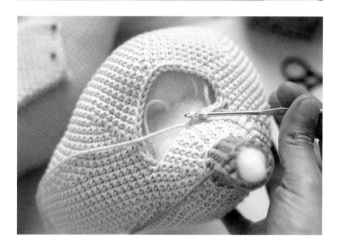

Rnd 16 – 17: sc in all 8 st [8]
Fasten off, leaving a long tail. Stuff the feet a bit more. Using a tapestry needle, weave the yarn tail through the front loop of each remaining stitch

and pull tight to close. Weave in the yarn end.
Sew the feet to the legs.

WINGS

(make 2, in cream)
Start with the feathers.

SMALL FEATHER
Rnd 1: start 5 sc in a magic ring [5]
Rnd 2: inc in all 5 st [10]
Rnd 3 – 5: sc in all 10 st [10]
Fasten off, leaving a tail for sewing.

MEDIUM FEATHER
Rnd 1: start 6 sc in a magic ring [6]
Rnd 2: inc in all 6 st [12]
Rnd 3 – 7: sc in all 12 st [12]
Fasten off, leaving a tail for sewing.

LARGE FEATHER
Rnd 1: start 7 sc in a magic ring [7]
Rnd 2: inc in all 7 st [14]
Rnd 3 – 9: sc in all 14 st [14]
Do not fasten off, as we will be joining the
feathers to make the wing.
Rnd 10: sc in next 6 st on the medium feather,
sc in all 10 st on the small feather, sc in left-
over 6 st on the medium feather, sc in all 14 st
on the large feather [36]
You can sew the holes between the feathers
closed using the leftover yarn tails and your
tapestry needle.
Rnd 11: sc in all 36 st [36]
Rnd 12: sc in next 27 st, dec 2 times, sc in next
5 st [34]
Rnd 13: sc in all 34 st [34]
Rnd 14: sc in next 26 st, dec 2 times, sc in next
4 st [32]
Rnd 15: sc in all 32 st [32]

Rnd 16: sc in next 25 st, dec 2 times, sc in next 3 st [30]
Rnd 17: sc in all 30 st [30]
Rnd 18: sc in next 24 st, dec 2 times, sc in next 2 st [28]
Rnd 19: sc in all 28 st [28]
Rnd 20: sc in next 23 st, dec 2 times, sc in next st [26]
Rnd 21: sc in all 26 st [26]
Rnd 22: sc in next 22 st, dec 2 times [24]
Rnd 23: sc in all 24 st [24]
Rnd 24: (sc in next 4 st, dec) repeat 4 times [20]
Fasten off, leaving a long tail for sewing. The wings
do not need to be stuffed. Flatten and sew the wings
to both sides between rounds 34 and 44.

COMB

(in brick red)

LARGE PART
Rnd 1: start 6 sc in a magic ring [6]
Rnd 2: inc in all 6 st [12]
Rnd 3: (sc in next st, inc in next st) repeat 6 times [18]
Rnd 4: (sc in next 2 st, inc in next st) repeat 6
times [24]
Rnd 5 – 7: sc in all 24 st [24]
Rnd 8: (sc in next 4 st, dec) repeat 4 times [20]
Rnd 9 – 10: sc in all 20 st [20]
Fasten off, leaving a long tail for sewing. Do not stuff.

MEDIUM PART
Rnd 1: start 6 sc in a magic ring [6]
Rnd 2: inc in all 6 st [12]
Rnd 3: (sc in next st, inc in next st) repeat 6 times [18]
Rnd 4 – 6: sc in all 18 st [18]
Rnd 7: (sc in next 4 st, dec) repeat 3 times [15]
Rnd 8: sc in all 15 st [15]
Fasten off, leaving a long tail for sewing. Do not stuff.

SMALL PART
Rnd 1: start 6 sc in a magic ring [6]
Rnd 2: inc in all 6 st [12]

Rnd 3 – 5: sc in all 12 st [12]
Fasten off, leaving a long tail for sewing. Do not stuff.

Flatten the parts of the comb and sew them to the top of the head. Sew the large part between rounds 4 and 5, the medium part behind the large part, between rounds 3 and 4, and the small part behind the medium part, between rounds 2 and 3.

TAIL FEATHERS

LARGE FEATHER
(start in graphite gray)
Rnd 1: start 6 sc in a magic ring [6]
Continue working in a stripe pattern, changing color every round, alternating cream and graphite gray yarn.
Rnd 2: inc in all 6 st [12]
Rnd 3: (sc in next st, inc in next st) repeat 6 times [18]
Rnd 4 – 9: sc in all 18 st [18]
Rnd 10: (sc in next 4 st, dec) repeat 3 times [15]
Rnd 11 – 12: sc in all 15 st [15]
Rnd 13: (sc in next 3 st, dec) repeat 3 times [12]
Rnd 14 – 15: sc in all 12 st [12]
Fasten off, leaving a long tail for sewing.

SMALL FEATHER
(make 2, start in graphite gray)
Rnd 1: start 8 sc in a magic ring [8]
Continue working in a stripe pattern, changing color every round, alternating cream and graphite gray yarn.
Rnd 2: inc in all 8 st [16]
Rnd 3 – 8: sc in all 16 st [16]
Rnd 9: (sc in next 2 st, dec) repeat 4 times [12]
Rnd 10 – 11: sc in all 12 st [12]
Fasten off, leaving a long tail for sewing. The feathers do not need to be stuffed.
Flatten and sew the feathers to the back, the large one centered between rounds 32 and 33. Sew the smaller ones on each side of the large feather.

143

SHAWL

(using a size C-2 / 2.75 mm or a D-3 / 3.25 mm hook for a more fluid piece, in pastel mint)
Ch 6. Crochet in rows.
Row 1: start in sixth ch from the hook, dc in this st, ch 3, turn.
Row 2: 6 dc in next ch 3-space, ch 6, turn.
Row 3: skip 2 st, sc in next 3 st, ch 3, skip 1 st, dc in the ch-3 turn ch, ch 3, turn.
Row 4: 5 dc in next ch-3 space, skip 1 st, sc in next st, skip 1 st, 6 dc in next ch-3 space, ch 6, turn.
Row 5: skip 2 st, sc in next 3 st, ch 3, skip 3 st, sc in next 3 st, ch 3, skip 1 st, dc in next ch-3 space, ch 3, turn.
Row 6: (5 dc in next ch-3 space, skip 1 st, sc in next st, skip 1 st) repeat 2 times, 6 dc in next ch-3 space ch 6, turn.
Row 7: skip 2 st, sc in next 3 st, (ch 3, skip 3 st, sc in next 3 st) repeat 2 times, ch 3, skip 1 st, dc in next ch-3-space, ch 3, turn.
Row 8: (5 dc in next ch-3 space, skip 1 st, sc in next st, skip 1 st) repeat 3 times, 6 dc in next ch-3 space ch 6, turn.
Row 9: skip 2 st, sc in next 3 st, (ch 3, skip 3 st, sc in next 3 st) repeat 3 times, ch 3, skip 1 st, dc in next ch-3-space, ch 3, turn.
Row 10: (5 dc in next ch-3 space, skip 1 st, sc in next st, skip 1 st) repeat 4 times, 6 dc in next ch-3 space, ch 1. Do not turn.
Do not fasten off. Continue making the edging.

EDGING

Row 1: crochet 30 sc down the first side (3 sc per dc, 3 sc per ch-3-space), ch 1, crochet 30 sc up the second side, ch 4, turn.
Row 2: skip 3 st, sc in next 3 st, (ch 3, skip 3 st, sc in next 3 st) repeat 4 times, ch 3, skip 1 ch, (sc in next 3 st, ch 3, skip 3 st) repeat 5 times, sc in next ch, ch 3, turn.
Row 3: 4 dc in next ch-3 space, skip 1 st, sc in next st, skip 1 st, (5 dc in next ch-3 space,

skip 1 st, sc in next st, skip 1 st) repeat 4 times, 6 dc in next ch-3 space (the bottom corner, the tip of the shawl), skip 1 st, sc in next st, skip 1 st, (5 dc in next ch-3 space, skip 1 st, sc in next st, skip 1 st) repeat 4 times, 5 dc in last ch-3 space.
Do not fasten off. Continue making the straps.

STRAPS

For the straps, ch 25, start in second ch from the hook, slst in next 24 st, slst across the top (about 38 st), ch 25 to make the other strap, start in second ch from the hook, slst in next 24 st, slst in the stitch where the foundation chain starts. Fasten off and weave in the yarn ends.

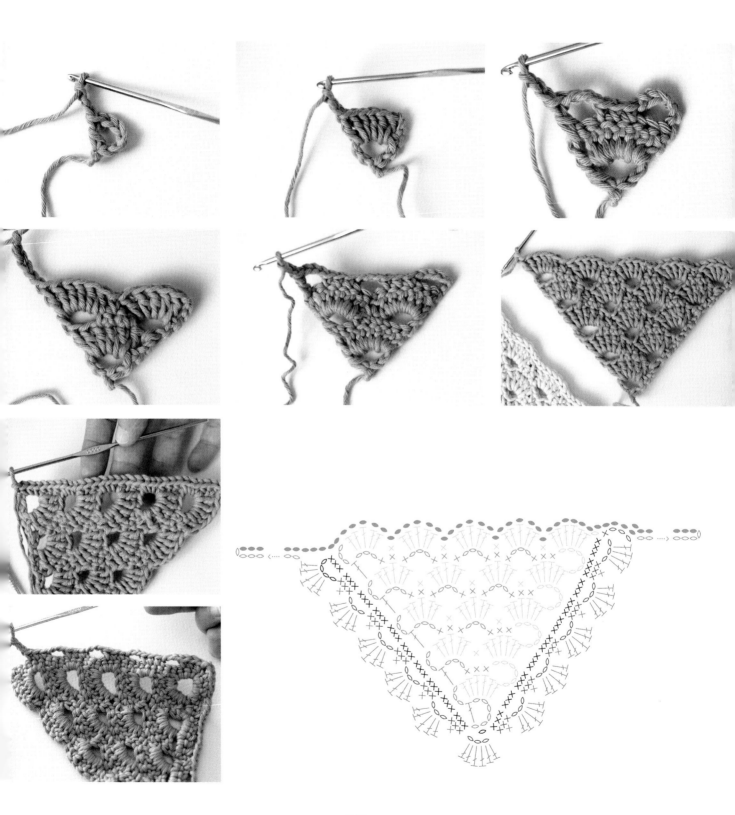

Cosmo Snail

Cosmo is a Botanist, a plant scientist. Plants are his passion. Especially flowers. Especially edible flowers. In recent years, he got excited about bakery as well. First, he was only interested in eating cakes, but now he's also keen on making them. At first, he tried baking a cake on his own, but he soon discovered that not having hands could make some parts of the process, let's say, challenging... not to mention slimy. But Cosmo wasn't going to give up, so he partnered with his good old and giant friend, Eduardo Cutesaurus. Together they opened the first vegan bakery in town. That is, they only use plants to make delicious cakes. Obviously, adorned with the most beautiful edible flowers he knows.

GALLERY: Scan or visit *www.amigurumi.com/4116* to share pictures and find inspiration.

SKILL LEVEL **

Size:
11.5 inches / 29 cm tall when made with the indicated yarn (eye stalks included)

Materials:
– Worsted weight yarn in
  · aqua blue
  · pale pink
  · yellow
  · pastel pink (leftover)
  · off-white (leftover)
  · black (leftover)
– Size C-2 / 2.75 mm crochet hook
– Black safety eyes (10 mm)
– Tapestry needle
– Fiberfill

Skills needed: magic ring *(page 32)*, embroidery *(page 38)*, joining parts *(page 39)*, crochet an elongated back *(page 126)*, working tapestry crochet *(page 36)*, working jacquard crochet from a diagram *(page 36)*, crab stitch *(page 30)*

Note: The head and body are worked in one piece.

CHEEKS

(make 2, in pastel pink)
Rnd 1: start 6 sc in a magic ring [6]
Rnd 2: inc in all 6 st [12]
Fasten off, leaving a long tail for sewing.

EYE WHITES

(make 2, in off-white)
Rnd 1: start 8 sc loosely in a magic ring [8]
Do not close the ring too tightly. Slst in next st. Fasten off, leaving a long tail for sewing. Insert the safety eyes in the center of the eye whites, but do not close the washers yet.

HEAD AND BODY

(start in aqua blue)
Start with the eye stalks, make 2.
Rnd 1: start 7 sc in a magic ring [7]
Rnd 2: inc in all 7 st [14]
Rnd 3 – 7: sc in all 14 st [14]
Insert the safety eye with the eye white

between rounds 4 and 5. Close the washer and sew the eye white to the eye stalk.
Rnd 8 – 16: sc in all 14 st [14]
Fasten off and weave in the yarn end on the first eye stalk. Do not fasten off on the second eye stalk. We will be joining the eye stalks in the next round to make the head.
Note: Start the next round at the side of the eye stalk. If you're not there yet, crochet a few more sc on the eye stalk or undo them until you reach that point. Make sure that both eyes are facing in the same direction while joining them.
Rnd 17: ch 4, sc in next 14 st on the first eye stalk, sc in next 4 ch, sc in next 14 st on the second eye stalk, sc in next 4 ch [36]
Rnd 18: (sc in next 5 st, inc in next st) repeat 6 times [42]
Rnd 19 – 20: sc in all 42 st [42]
Rnd 21: (sc in next 6 st, inc in next st) repeat 6 times [48]
Rnd 22 – 27: sc in all 48 st [48]
Embroider the mouth between rounds 19 and 20 with black yarn. Sew the cheeks between rounds 17 and 21. Stuff the eye stalks lightly and continue stuffing as you go.
Rnd 28: (sc in next 7 st, inc in next st) repeat 6 times [54]
Rnd 29 – 32: sc in all 54 st [54]

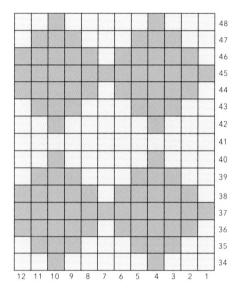

												48
												47
												46
												45
												44
												43
												42
												41
												40
												39
												38
												37
												36
												35
												34
12	11	10	9	8	7	6	5	4	3	2	1	

Change to pale pink.
Rnd 33: sc in all 54 st [54]
Continue working in a jacquard pattern, alternating yellow and pale pink yarn according to the diagram.
Rnd 34 – 48: sc in all 54 st [54]
Continue in pale pink yarn.
Rnd 49: sc in all 54 st [54]
Change to aqua blue.
Rnd 50: BLO sc in all 54 [54]
Rnd 51: sc in next 12 st. Find the side of the body. If you are not there yet, crochet a few more sc or undo them. Then, ch 17. (Place a stitch marker in the next st you make – the first you will make on the foundation chain, this will mark the beginning of the next rounds.) Crochet back on the chain, inc in second ch from hook, sc in next 15 st, sc in the stitch where the foun-

dation chain starts, continue on the body and sc in next 54 st, continue on the other side of the chain and sc in next 16 st [88]
Rnd 52: inc in next 2 st, sc in next 85 st, inc in next st [91]
Rnd 53: (sc in next st, inc in next st) repeat 2 times, sc in next 86 st, inc in next st [94]
Rnd 54 – 57: sc in all 94 st [94]
Rnd 58: sc in next 4 st, dec, sc in next 84 st, dec, sc in next 2 st [92]

Rnd 59: sc in next 4 st, dec, sc in next 34 st, dec, sc in next 10 st, dec, sc in next 34 st, dec, sc in next 2 st [88]
Rnd 60: sc in next 4 st, dec, sc in next 32 st, dec, sc in next 10 st, dec, sc in next 32 st, dec, sc in next 2 st [84]
Rnd 61: sc in next 4 st, dec, sc in next 30 st, dec, sc in next 10 st, dec, sc in next 30 st, dec, sc in next 2 st [80]
Rnd 62: sc in next 4 st, dec, sc in

next 28 st, dec, sc in next 10 st, dec, sc in next 28 st, dec, sc in next 2 st [76]

Rnd 63: sc in next 4 st, dec, sc in next 26 st, dec, sc in next 10 st, dec, sc in next 26 st, dec, sc in next 2 st [72]

Rnd 64: (sc in next 4 st, dec) repeat 12 times [60]

Rnd 65: (sc in next 8 st, dec) repeat 6 times [54]

Rnd 66: (sc in next 7 st, dec) repeat 6 times [48]
Stuff the head and the body firmly. Continue stuffing as you go.

Rnd 67: (sc in next 6 st, dec) repeat 6 times [42]

Rnd 68: (sc in next 5 st, dec) repeat 6 times [36]

Rnd 69: (sc in next 4 st, dec) repeat 6 times [30]

Rnd 70: (sc in next 3 st, dec) repeat 6 times [24]

Rnd 71: (sc in next 2 st, dec) repeat 6 times [18]

Rnd 72: (sc in next st, dec) repeat 6 times [12]

Rnd 73: dec 6 times [6]
Fasten off, leaving a long tail. Using a tapestry needle, weave the yarn tail through the front loop of each remaining stitch and pull tight to close. Weave in the yarn end.

FOOT

(start in aqua blue)
Leave a long starting yarn tail. Ch 80. Make sure your chain isn't twisted. Insert the hook in the first chain stitch and join the foundation chain with a slst. Continue working in a spiral.

Rnd 1: sc in all 80 st [80]

Rnd 2: inc in all 80 st [160]

Rnd 3: (sc in next 7 st, inc in next st) repeat 20 times [180]
Change to pale pink yarn.

Rnd 4: (sc in next 11 st, inc in next st) repeat 15 times [195]
Change to yellow yarn.

Rnd 5: (sc in next 12 st, inc in next st) repeat 15 times [210]

Rnd 6: ch 1, crab stitch in all 210 st [210]
Fasten off and weave in the yarn end.
Pin the foot all around the snail body (as if you were putting on a skirt), over rounds 60 and 63 and sew it on with the aqua blue starting yarn tail.

Note: It's not going to be a straight line. Do take into account that the foot is going to help the snail stand up.

SHELL

Note: I use the jacquard crochet technique for the shell. Alternatively, you can also use the tapestry technique. If you are not confident using these techniques, you can choose to crochet the shell in one color or in a horizontal stripe pattern.

Note: The shell is made with two parts that are sewn together.

SHELL PART 1
(start in yellow yarn)
Rnd 1: start 8 sc in a magic ring [8]
Continue working with alternating yarns (yellow and pale pink). Work the second stitch in each increase in pale pink yarn. You will have 8 pale pink lines.
Rnd 2: inc in all 8 st [16]
Rnd 3: (sc in next st, inc in next st) repeat 8 times [24]
Rnd 4: (sc in next 2 st, inc in next st) repeat 8 times [32]
Rnd 5: (sc in next 3 st, inc in next st) repeat 8 times [40]
Rnd 6: (sc in next 4 st, inc in next st) repeat 8 times [48]
Rnd 7: (sc in next 5 st, inc in next st) repeat 8 times [56]
Rnd 8: (sc in next 6 st, inc in next st) repeat 8 times [64]
Continue in pale pink yarn.
Rnd 9: (sc in next 7 st, inc in next st) repeat 8 times [72]
Change to yellow yarn.
Rnd 10: BLO sc in all 72 st [72]
Rnd 11 – 15: sc in all 72 st [72]
Fasten off and weave in the yarn end.

SHELL PART 2
(start in yellow yarn)
Rnd 1 – 9: repeat the pattern for the first shell part.
Fasten off, leaving a long tail for sewing.

SMALL CENTER BUTTON
(make 2, in yellow yarn)
Rnd 1: start 8 sc in a magic ring [8]
Rnd 2: sc in all 8 st [8]
Fasten off, leaving a long tail for sewing. Do not stuff.

ASSEMBLY OF THE SHELL
Using a tapestry needle and the yarn tail of the second shell part, sew both parts together using

the whip stitch. Insert the needle underneath both loops of the first shell part (the yellow stitches) and the back loop only of the second shell part (the pale pink stitches). We are going to use the leftover front loops on the second shell part for an extra round of slst. Stuff the shell before closing the seam. Do not overstuff, we want the shell to be fluffy and flat like a cushion.

Rejoin the pale pink yarn in a leftover front loop of round 9 of the first shell part, slst in all 72 st. Fasten off and weave in the yarn end. Repeat on the other side, in the leftover front loops of your whip stitch seam.

Sew the button to the center of the first part. Pass the needle through to the other side to pull the button slightly inwards. Repeat with the second button on the other shell part.

Sew the shell centered to the back, over round 55.

Angelica Whale

Angelica is a blue whale, and if you missed the fact, the largest known animal to have ever lived. Yes, larger than dinosaurs. Please, don't tell Eduardo Cutesaurus, he thinks he's the largest. Luckily Angelica doesn't care about numbers at all. Angelica is a speech therapist. She helps clients to improve their communication when they have difficulty speaking up, listening or finding the right words to vent their hearts. Despite the fact that they live in different worlds, one of her dearest friends is Greta Hen. And Greta insisted on crocheting her a present. Probably centimeters and meters were swapped at some point in the conversation... miscommunication happens even to a speech therapist. But Angelica doesn't care about the small size of her crocheted hat, which she wears with pride!

GALLERY: Scan or visit *www.amigurumi.com/4117* to share pictures and find inspiration.

Note: Use a size C-2 / 2.75 mm crochet hook, unless otherwise noted.

Note: Alike all my toys, this design was made using the X-shaped single crochet stitch. If you use V-shaped stitches, the line between color changes will start to turn. A perfectly straight line is impossible, as even X-shaped stitches make your line turn at some point. So don't worry too much about it.

HEAD AND BODY

(start in petrol blue)
Ch 8. Stitches are worked around both sides of the foundation chain.
Rnd 1: start in second ch from the hook, inc in this st, sc in next 5 st, 3 sc in last st. Continue on the other side of the foundation chain, sc in next 6 st [16]
Rnd 2: inc in next 2 st, sc in next 5 st, inc in next 3 st, sc in next 5 st, inc in next st [22]
Continue working with alternating yarns (petrol blue and off-white). The color you work with is indicated before each part.
Rnd 3: *(petrol blue)* sc in next 14 st, *(off-white)* (sc in next st, inc in next st) repeat 4 times [26]
Rnd 4: *(petrol blue)* sc in next 14 st, *(off-white)* sc in next 12 st [26]
Rnd 5: *(petrol blue)* (sc in next 2 st, inc in next st) repeat 4 times, sc in next 2 st, *(off-white)* (sc in next 2 st, inc in next st) repeat 4 times [34]
Rnd 6 – 7: *(petrol blue)* sc in next 18 st, *(off-white)* sc in next 16 st [34]
Rnd 8: *(petrol blue)* sc in next 18 st, *(off-white)* sc in next 6 st, inc in next 4 st, sc in next 6 st [38]

152

Rnd 9 – 10: *(petrol blue)* sc in next 18 st, *(off-white)* sc in next 20 st [38]

Rnd 11: *(petrol blue)* sc in next st, inc in next st, sc in next 14 st, inc in next st, sc in next st, *(off-white)* sc in next 7 st, (inc in next st, sc in next st) repeat 3 times, inc in next st, sc in next 6 st [44]

Rnd 12 – 14: *(petrol blue)* sc in next 20 st, *(off-white)* sc in next 24 st [44]

Rnd 15: *(petrol blue)* sc in next st, inc in next st, sc in next 16 st, inc in next st, sc in next st, *(off-white)* sc in next 7 st, (inc in next st, sc in next 2 st) repeat 3 times, inc in next st, sc in next 7 st [50]

Rnd 16 – 18: *(petrol blue)* sc in next 22 st, *(off-white)* sc in next 28 st [50]

Rnd 19: *(petrol blue)* sc in next st, inc in next st, sc in next 18 st, inc in next st, sc in next st, *(off-white)* sc in next 9 st, (inc in next st, sc in next 2 st) repeat 3 times, inc in next st, sc in next 9 st [56]

Rnd 20 – 22: *(petrol blue)* sc in next 24 st, *(off-white)* sc in next 32 st [56]

Rnd 23: *(petrol blue)* sc in next 24 st, *(off-white)* sc in next 28 st, *(petrol blue)* sc in next 4 st [56]

Rnd 24: *(petrol blue)* sc in next 28 st, *(off-white)* sc in next 8 st, inc in next st, sc in next st, inc in next st, sc in next 2 st, inc in next st, sc in next st, inc in next st, sc in next 7 st, *(petrol blue)* sc in next 5 st [60]

Rnd 25: *(petrol blue)* sc in next 29 st, *(off-white)* sc in next 25 st, *(petrol blue)* sc in next 6 st [60]

Rnd 26: *(petrol blue)* sc in next 30 st, *(off-white)* sc in next 23 st, *(petrol blue)* sc in next 7 st [60]

Rnd 27: *(petrol blue)* sc in next 31 st, *(off-white)* sc in next 21 st, *(petrol blue)* sc in next 8 st [60]

Rnd 28 – 58: *(petrol blue)* sc in next 32 st, *(off-white)* sc in next 20 st, *(petrol blue)* sc in next 8 st [60] Insert the safety eyes between rounds 29 and 30, about 4 stitches from the off-white patch. Embroider the cheeks below the eyes with pastel pink yarn. Stuff the head and continue stuffing as you go.

Rnd 59: *(petrol blue)* sc in next 32 st, *(off-white)* sc in next 4 st, dec, sc in next st, dec, sc in next 2 st, dec, sc in next st, dec, sc in next 4 st, *(petrol blue)* sc in next 8 st [56]

Rnd 60: *(petrol blue)* sc in next 32 st, *(off-white)* sc in next 16 st, *(petrol blue)* sc in next 8 st [56]

Rnd 61: *(petrol blue)* sc in next 32 st, *(off-white)* sc in next 5 st, dec, sc in next 2 st, dec, sc in next 5 st, *(petrol blue)* sc in next 8 st [54]

Rnd 62: *(petrol blue)* sc in next 32 st, *(off-white)* sc in next 14 st, *(petrol blue)* sc in next 8 st [54]

Rnd 63: *(petrol blue)* sc in next 32 st, *(off-white)* sc in next 3 st, dec, sc in next 4 st, dec, sc in next 3 st, *(petrol blue)* sc in next 8 st [52]

Rnd 64: *(petrol blue)* sc in next 29 st, dec, sc in next st, *(off-white)* sc in next 12 st, *(petrol blue)* sc in next st, dec, sc in next 5 st [50]

Rnd 65: *(petrol blue)* sc in next 31 st, *(off-white)* sc in next 4 st, dec 2 times, sc in next 4 st, *(petrol blue)* sc in next 7 st [48]

Rnd 66: *(petrol blue)* sc in next 28 st, dec, sc in next st, *(off-white)* sc in next 10 st, *(petrol blue)* sc in next st, dec, sc in next 4 st [46]

Rnd 67: *(petrol blue)* sc in next 30 st, *(off-white)* (sc in next 2 st, dec) repeat 2 times, sc in next 2 st, *(petrol blue)* sc in next 6 st [44]

Rnd 68: *(petrol blue)* sc in next 27 st, dec, sc in next st, *(off-white)* sc in next 8 st, *(petrol blue)* sc in next st, dec, sc in next 3 st [42]

Rnd 69: *(petrol blue)* sc in next 29 st, *(off-white)* sc in next 2 st, dec 2 times, sc in next 2 st, *(petrol blue)* sc in next 5 st [40]

Rnd 70: *(petrol blue)* sc in next 26 st, dec, sc in next st, *(off-white)* sc in next 6 st, *(petrol blue)* sc in next st, dec, sc in next 2 st [38]

Rnd 71: *(petrol blue)* sc in next 28 st, *(off-white)* sc in next st, dec 2 times, sc in next st, *(petrol blue)* sc in next 4 st [36]

Rnd 72: *(petrol blue)* sc in next 25 st, dec, sc in next st, *(off-white)* sc in next 4 st, *(petrol blue)* sc in next st, dec, sc in next st [34]

Rnd 73: *(petrol blue)* sc in next 27 st, *(off-white)* dec 2 times, *(petrol blue)* sc in next 3 st [32] Continue in petrol blue yarn.

Rnd 74: sc in next 24 st, dec, sc in next 4 st, dec [30]

Rnd 75: sc in all 30 st [30]

Rnd 76: sc in next 24 st, dec, sc in next 4 st [29]

Rnd 77: dec, sc in next 27 st [28]

Rnd 78: sc in all 28 st [28]

Rnd 79: sc in next 24 st, dec 2 times [26]

Rnd 80: sc in next 26 st [26]

Rnd 81: sc in next 2 st, dec, sc in next 18 st, dec, sc in next

2 st [24]

Rnd 82: sc in all 24 st [24]
Rnd 83: sc in next st, dec, sc in next 18 st, dec, sc in next st [22]
Rnd 84: sc in all 22 st [22]
Rnd 85: dec, sc in next 18 st, dec [20]
Rnd 86: sc in all 20 st [20]
Rnd 87: sc in next st, dec, sc in next 14 st, dec, sc in next st [18]
Rnd 88 – 89: sc in all 18 st [18]
Rnd 90: (sc in next st, dec) repeat 6 times [12]
Rnd 91: dec 6 times [6]
Fasten off, leaving a long tail. Using a tapestry needle, weave the yarn tail through the front loop of each remaining stitch and pull tight to close. Weave in the yarn end.

VENTRAL PLEATS
(in off-white)
Note: The ventral pleats are optional, if you prefer your whale without them, you can leave them out.
The first ventral pleat will be positioned at 3 or 4 stitches from the petrol blue top of the snout. Insert the hook between rounds 2 and 3, and pull up a loop of off-white yarn. Make a surface slst. Then, insert the hook in the next stitch, between rounds 3 and 4 of the belly, draw up a loop and make a surface slst. Continue making surface slst until you reach the petrol blue edge at the end of the whale body. Fasten off and weave in the yarn end.
Make another 6 ventral pleats in the same way.

TAIL

(in petrol blue)
Rnd 1: start 5 sc in a magic ring [5]
Rnd 2: inc in all 5 st [10]
Rnd 3: inc in all 10 st [20]
Rnd 4: (sc in next st, inc in next st) repeat 10 times [30]
Rnd 5: (sc in next 2 st, inc in next st) repeat 10 times [40]
Rnd 6: (sc in next 3 st, inc in next st) repeat 10 times [50]
Rnd 7: (sc in next 4 st, inc in next st) repeat 10 times [60]
Rnd 8: (sc in next 5 st, inc in next st) repeat 10 times [70]
Rnd 9: (sc in next 6 st, inc in next st) repeat 10 times [80]
Rnd 10: (sc in next 7 st, inc in next st) repeat 10 times [90]
Rnd 11: sc in all 90 st [90]

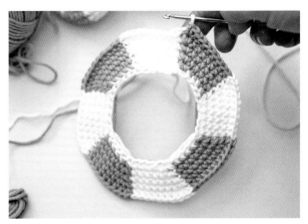

Do not fasten off. Fold the tail closed. Flatten the tail and work the next round through both layers to close. The tail does not need to be stuffed.
Rnd 12: slst in all 45 st [45]
Fasten off and weave in the yarn end. Sew the tail over rounds 89 to 91.

FLIPPERS

(make 2, in petrol blue)
Rnd 1: start 6 sc in a magic ring [6]
Rnd 2: sc in all 6 st [6]
Rnd 3: sc in next st, inc in next st, sc in next 4 st [7]
Rnd 4: sc in all 7 st [7]
Rnd 5: sc in next 2 st, inc in next st, sc in next 4 st [8]
Rnd 6: sc in all 8 st [8]
Rnd 7: sc in next 3 st, inc in next st, sc in next 4 st [9]
Rnd 8: sc in all 9 st [9]
Rnd 9: sc in next 3 st, inc in next st, sc in next st, inc in next st, sc in next 3 st [11]
Rnd 10 – 11: sc in all 11 st [11]
Rnd 12: sc in next 4 st, inc in next st, sc in next st, inc in next st, sc in next 4 st [13]
Rnd 13 – 14: sc in all 13 st [13]
Rnd 15: sc in next 5 st, inc in next st, sc in next st, inc in next st, sc in next 5 st [15]
Note: In the next rounds we add the bobbles on the flippers. These don't have a fixed position. Cro-

chet a bobble in every few rounds, positioning them a few stitches apart on the right side of the flipper.

Rnd 16 – 32: sc in all 15 st, fitfully making a 5-dc-bobble st on the right side of the flipper [15]

Rnd 33 – 34: sc in all 15 st [15]

Fasten off, leaving a long tail for sewing. The flippers do not need to be stuffed. Flatten and sew the flippers to both sides between rounds 34 and 41, right next to the off-white belly.

LIFEBUOY

(start in cream)

Ch 40. Make sure your chain isn't twisted. Insert the hook in the first chain stitch and join the foundation chain with a slst. Continue working in spiral, alternating cream and pastel pink yarn. The color you work with is indicated before each part.

Rnd 1: ((*cream*) sc in next 4 st, inc in next st, (*pastel pink*) sc in next 4 st, inc in next st) repeat 4 times [48]

Rnd 2: ((*cream*) sc in next 5 st, inc in next st, (*pastel pink*) sc in next 5 st, inc in next st) repeat 4 times [56]

Rnd 3: ((*cream*) sc in next 6 st, inc in next st, (*pastel pink*) sc in next 6 st, inc in next st) repeat 4 times [64]

Rnd 4: ((*cream*) sc in next 7 st, inc in next st, (*pastel pink*) sc in next 7 st, inc in next st) repeat 4 times [72]

Rnd 5: ((*cream*) sc in next 8 st, inc in next st, (*pastel pink*) sc in next 8 st, inc in next st) repeat 4 times [80]

Rnd 6 – 15: ((*cream*) sc in next 10 st, (*pastel pink*) sc in next 10 st) repeat 4 times [80]

Rnd 16: ((*cream*) dec, sc in next 8 st, (*pastel pink*) dec, sc in next 8 st) repeat 4 times [72]

Rnd 17: ((*cream*) dec, sc in next 7 st, (*pastel pink*) dec, sc in next 7 st) repeat 4 times [64]

Rnd 18: ((*cream*) dec, sc in next 6 st, (*pastel pink*) dec, sc in next 6 st) repeat 4 times [56]

Rnd 19: ((*cream*) dec, sc in next 5 st, (*pastel pink*) dec, sc in next 5 st) repeat 4 times [48]

Rnd 20: ((*cream*) dec, sc in next 4 st, (*pastel pink*) dec, sc in next 4 st) repeat 4 times [40]

Fasten off, leaving a long tail for sewing. Sew round 20 to round 1 to make a ring. Stuff as you go.

MINI HAT

(with fingering weight yarn, using a B-1 / 2 mm crochet hook, in pastel pink)

Repeat the pattern for Alberto Seagull's hat on page 128.

FAKE POMPON OR MINI BALL
(with fingering weight yarn, using a B-1 / 2 mm crochet hook, start in pastel pink)

Rnd 1: start 6 sc in a magic ring [6]

Change to cream yarn.

Rnd 2: inc in all 6 st [12]

Continue in a stripe pattern, changing color every round, alternating pastel pink and off-white yarn.

Rnd 3: (sc in next st, inc in next st) repeat 6 times [18]

Rnd 4 – 6: sc in all 18 st [18]

Rnd 7: (sc in next st, dec) repeat 6 times [12]

Stuff lightly.

Rnd 8: dec 6 times [6]

Fasten off, leaving a long tail for sewing. Sew the pompon to the top of the hat.

Roberto Dachshund

If you look for the word "joy" in the dictionary, you'll likely come across Roberto's photo. He typically has a smile drawn on his face and walks through life giving a paw to everyone who needs it. He is the best at listening and has the beautiful talent to find a silver lining in any situation. And he loves Italian food. So, it's no surprise that he chose to work in a lovely 'minusculo' hotel in Italy, where he receives guests with his big smile, chats with everyone he meets, helps guests tick off their bucket-list travel experiences, and gives tips on where to eat the best Italian food. We could say that the only flaw Roberto has, is his irremediable love for garlic, which could be a bit of a problem when your work is accommodating people all day long.

 GALLERY: Scan or visit *www.amigurumi.com/4118* to share pictures and find inspiration.

SKILL LEVEL *

Size:
8 inches / 20 cm tall and
12 inches / 30 cm long when
made with the indicated yarn

Materials:
– Worsted weight yarn in
  · mustard yellow
  · black
  · off-white
  · teal green
– Size C-2 / 2.75 mm
  crochet hook
– Black oval safety eyes
  (12 mm)
– Tapestry needle
– Fiberfill

Skills needed: magic ring
(page 32), changing color
at the beginning of a round
(page 35), dividing the body
in four parts *(explained in
pattern)*, backstitch *(page
38)*, joining parts *(page 39)*,
embroidery *(page 38)*

Note: *The head, body and legs are worked in one piece.*

HEAD

(start in black)
Start with the nose.
Rnd 1: start 6 sc in a magic ring [6]
Rnd 2: inc in all 6 st [12]
Rnd 3 – 6: sc in all 12 st [12]
Change to mustard yellow yarn.
Note: When fastening off the black yarn, you can leave a long yarn tail to embroider the mouth later on.
Rnd 7: (sc in next st, inc in next st) repeat 6 times [18]
Rnd 8 – 11: sc in all 18 st [18]
Rnd 12: sc in next 8 st, inc in next 2 st, sc in next 8 st [20]
Rnd 13 – 14: sc in all 20 st [20]
Rnd 15: sc in next 9 st, inc in next st, sc in next st, inc in next st, sc in next 8 st [22]
Rnd 16 – 17: sc in all 22 st [22]
Rnd 18: sc in next 10 st, inc in next st, sc in next 2 st, inc in next st, sc in next 8 st [24]
Rnd 19 – 20: sc in all 24 st [24]
Rnd 21: sc in next 7 st, (inc in next st, sc in next st) repeat 5 times, inc in next st, sc in next 6 st [30]
Rnd 22: sc in all 30 st [30]
Rnd 23: sc in next 8 st, (inc in next st, sc in next 2 st) repeat 5 times, inc in next st, sc in next 6 st [36]
Rnd 24: sc in all 36 st [36]
Rnd 25: sc in next 9 st, (inc in next st, sc in next 3 st) repeat 5 times, inc in next st, sc in next 6 st [42]
Rnd 26 – 27: sc in all 42 st [42]
Embroider the mouth with black yarn: make 15 vertical backstitches over rounds 7 to 21 and 10 horizonal backstitches between rounds 21 and 22. Stuff the nose.
Rnd 28: sc in next 10 st, (inc in next st, sc in next 4 st) repeat 5 times, inc in next st, sc in next 6 st [48]
Rnd 29 – 35: sc in all 48 st [48]
Insert the safety eyes between rounds 26 and 27, with an interspace of about 20 stitches at the top.
Rnd 36: (sc in next 6 st, dec) repeat 6 times [42]
Rnd 37: sc in all 42 st [42]
Rnd 38: (sc in next 5 st, dec) repeat 6 times [36]
Rnd 39: (sc in next 4 st, dec) repeat 6 times [30]
Rnd 40: (sc in next 3 st, dec) repeat 6 times [24]
Stuff the head firmly.
Rnd 41: (sc in next 2 st, dec) repeat 6 times [18]
Rnd 42: (sc in next st, dec) repeat 6 times [12]
Rnd 43: dec 6 times [6]

Fasten off, leaving a long tail. Using a tapestry needle, weave the yarn tail through the front loop of each remaining stitch and pull tight to close. Weave in the yarn end.

BODY

(start in mustard yellow)
Start with the neck. Leave a long starting yarn tail. Ch 20. Make sure your chain isn't twisted. Insert the hook in the first chain stitch and join the foundation chain with a slst. Continue working in a spiral.

Rnd 1 – 2: sc in all 20 st [20]
Continue in a stripe pattern, changing color every round, alternating off-white and teal green yarn.
Rnd 3: (sc in next 4 st, inc in next st) repeat 4 times [24]
Rnd 4 – 5: sc in all 24 st [24]
Rnd 6: (sc in next 5 st, inc in next st) repeat 4 times [28]
Rnd 7 – 9: sc in all 28 st [28]
Change to mustard yellow yarn.
Rnd 10: ch 31. (Place a stitch marker in the next st you make – the first you will make on the foundation chain, this will mark the beginning of the next rounds.) Crochet back on the chain, inc in second ch from the hook, sc in next 29 st, sc in the stitch where the foundation chain starts, continue on the neck and BLO sc in next 28 st, continue on the other side of the chain and sc in next 30 st [90]
Rnd 11: sc in next st, inc in next st, sc in next 87 st, inc in next st [92]
Rnd 12: sc in next 2 st, inc in next st, sc in next 88 st, inc in next st [94]
Rnd 13: sc in next 3 st, inc in next st, sc in next 89 st, inc in next st [96]
Rnd 14 – 20: sc in all 96 st [96]
Do not fasten off.

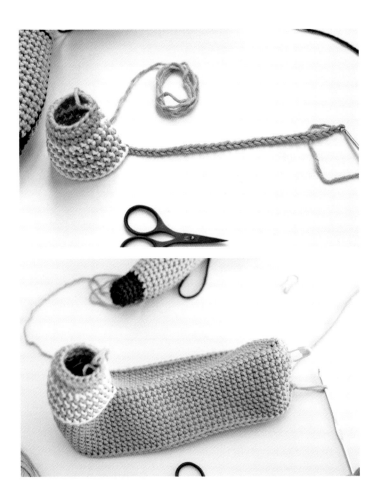

LEGS

We have to divide the work to crochet the four legs.

FIRST BACK LEG
First, find the middle back stitch of the body. If you are not there yet, continue crocheting until that point. Then, sc in next st. Place a stitch marker in the next stitch. Sc in next 9 st, ch 7. Join the last ch to the stitch with the stitch marker by working a slst. Continue working the first back leg:
Rnd 1: sc in next 9 st on the body, sc in next 7 ch [16]
Rnd 2 – 3: sc in all 16 st [16]
Rnd 4: (sc in next 6 st, dec) repeat 2 times [14]
Rnd 5: sc in all 14 st [14]
Rnd 6: (sc in next 5 st, dec) repeat 2 times [12]

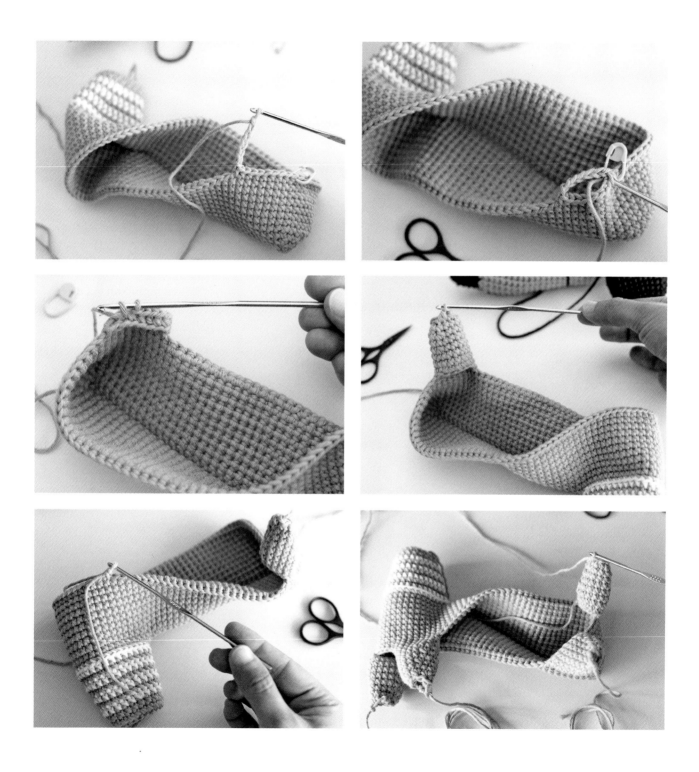

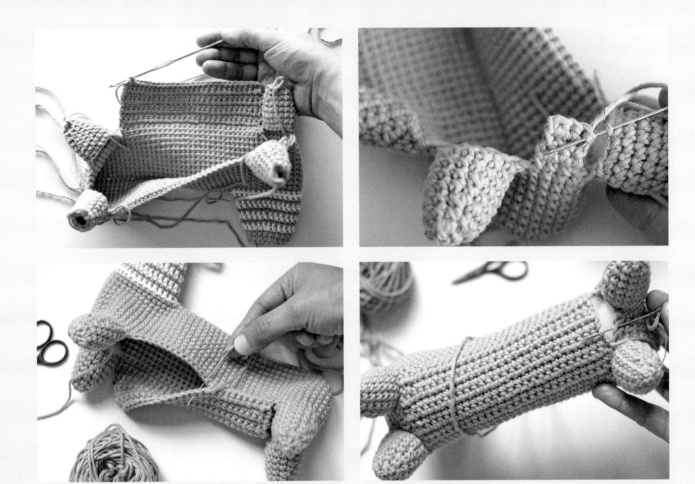

Rnd 7: sc in all 12 st [12]

Rnd 8: dec 6 times [6]

Fasten off, leaving a long tail. Using a tapestry needle, weave the yarn tail through the front loop of each remaining stitch and pull tight to close. Weave in the yarn end.

FIRST FRONT LEG

Count 27 stitches along from the first back leg (this will become the belly) and pull up a loop of mustard yellow yarn in the 28th stitch.

Sc in this st, sc in next 8 st, ch 7 and join the last ch to the first sc stitch with a slst.

Rnd 1 – 8: repeat rounds 1-8 of the first back leg.

SECOND FRONT LEG

Count 3 st to the left of the first front leg (this is the space between the legs) and pull up a loop of mustard yellow yarn in the 4th stitch.
Sc in this st, sc in next 8 st, ch 7 and join the last ch to the first sc stitch with a slst.
Rnd 1 – 8: repeat rounds 1-8 of the first back leg.

SECOND BACK LEG

Count 27 st to the left of the second front leg (this is the other side of the belly) and pull up a loop of mustard yellow yarn in the 28th stitch.
Sc in this st, sc in next 8 st, ch 7 and join the last ch to the first sc stitch with a slst.
Rnd 1 – 8: repeat rounds 1-8 of the first back leg.

BELLY

Between the legs you now have 27-stitch-spaces along the sides and 3-stitch-spaces at the front and back.
We make the belly by crocheting flaps on these stitches. Start with the 27 stitch spaces along the side. Pull up a loop of mustard yellow yarn in the first stitch next to the first leg you made. Crochet in rows.
Row 1 – 10: sc in next 27 st, ch 1, turn [27]
Fasten off, leaving a long tail for sewing.

FLAP BETWEEN THE LEGS

For the back flap, pull up a loop of mustard yellow yarn in the first stitch next to the last leg you made. Crochet in rows.
Row 1 – 4: sc in next 3 st, ch 1, turn [3]
Fasten off, leaving a long tail for sewing. Work the flap between the front legs in the same way.

ASSEMBLY OF THE BODY

Using a tapestry needle, sew the front flap to both front legs and the back flap to both back legs. Stuff each leg firmly. Using a tapestry needle, sew the wide belly flap to the opposite side of the dog's belly. Then sew the belly flap to both legs and the flaps between them, stuffing the body as you go. Sew the head to the body. If necessary, add more stuffing to the base of the neck before sewing the head on.
Note: You may notice that my dog's neck seems to have only one round in mustard yellow yarn before the stripe pattern, instead of two. I used the first round to sew the head to the body more firmly.

EARS

(make 2, in black)
Rnd 1: start 6 sc in a magic ring [6]
Rnd 2: inc in all 6 st [12]
Rnd 3: (sc in next st, inc in next st) repeat 6 times [18]
Rnd 4: sc in all 18 st [18]
Rnd 5: (sc in next 2 st, inc in next st) repeat 6 times [24]
Rnd 6 – 8: sc in all 24 st [24]
Rnd 9: (sc in next 4 st, dec) repeat 4 times [20]
Rnd 10 – 11: sc in all 20 st [20]
Rnd 12: (sc in next 3 st, dec) repeat 4 times [16]
Rnd 13 – 18: sc in all 16 st [16]
Fasten off, leaving a long tail for sewing. The ears do not need to be stuffed. Flatten the ears and sew them to rounds 29 to 36 of the head.

TAIL

(in black)
Rnd 1: start 5 sc in a magic ring st [5]
Rnd 2 – 4: sc in all 5 st [5]
Fasten off, leaving a long tail for sewing. The tail does not need to be stuffed. Sew the tail to the back, centered over rounds 10 and 11.

Amelia Giraffe

Amelia needs to know how things work. And for that she spends hours (re)assembling whatever objects she finds. She doesn't always manage to put things back together though, but she definitely tries. She wants to see everything, do everything and discover everything. But Amelia is afraid to fly and doesn't thrive on ships either. Her career as mechanical engineer does allow her to chat with pilots and sailors (and hear all about their trips and adventures) without sailing off with those terrifying (air)ships. But since Amelia learned about the mechanisms of all those marvelous vehicles, her next goal is to find the courage to make her first forays into both forms of travel and to finally discover the world.

GALLERY: Scan or visit www.amigurumi.com/4119 to share pictures and find inspiration.

SKILL LEVEL *

Size:
19.5 inches / 50 cm tall when made with the indicated yarn (horns included)

Materials:
– Worsted weight yarn in
  · light warm gray
  · off-white
  · graphite gray
  · pastel pink (leftover)
  · black
  · teal green
– Size C-2 / 2.75 mm crochet hook
– Tapestry needle
– Fiberfill

Skills needed: magic ring (page 32), dividing the body in four parts (page 160), work around a foundation chain (page 34), joining parts (page 39), embroidery (page 38)

Note: The head, body and legs are worked in one piece.

EYE WHITES

(make 2, in off-white)
Ch 5. Stitches are worked around both sides of the foundation chain.
Rnd 1: start in second ch from the hook, inc in this st, sc in next 2 st, 3 sc in last st. Continue on the other side of the foundation chain, sc in next 3 st [10]
Rnd 2: sc in next st, inc in next st, sc in next 2 st, inc in next st, sc in next st, inc in next st, sc in next 2 st, inc in last st [14]
Fasten off, leaving a long tail for sewing. Embroider the eye with black yarn.

SNOUT

(start in off-white)
Rnd 1: start 6 sc in a magic ring [6]
Rnd 2: inc in all 6 st [12]
Rnd 3: (sc in next st, inc in next st) repeat 6 times [18]
Rnd 4: (sc in next 2 st, inc in next st) repeat 6 times [24]
Rnd 5 – 6: sc in all 24 st [24]
Change to light warm gray yarn.
Rnd 7: sc in all 24 st [24]
Rnd 8: (sc in next 5 st, inc in next st) repeat 4 times [28]
Rnd 9 – 10: sc in all 28 st [28]
Rnd 11: (sc in next 6 st, inc in next st) repeat 4 times [32]
Rnd 12 – 13: sc in all 32 st [32]
Rnd 14: (sc in next 7 st, inc in next st) repeat 4 times [36]
Rnd 15: sc in all 36 st [36]
Fasten off, leaving a long tail for sewing. Embroider the nose and the mouth with black yarn. Stuff the snout with fiberfill.

HEAD AND BODY

(start in light warm gray)
Rnd 1: start 6 sc in a magic ring [6]
Rnd 2: inc in all 6 st [12]
Rnd 3: (sc in next st, inc in next st) repeat 6 times [18]

Rnd 4: (sc in next 2 st, inc in next st) repeat 6 times [24]
Rnd 5: (sc in next 3 st, inc in next st) repeat 6 times [30]
Rnd 6: (sc in next 4 st, inc in next st) repeat 6 times [36]
Rnd 7 – 20: sc in all 36 st [36]

Sew the snout between rounds 6 and 18. The snout must be placed on the opposite side of the start of the round.
Note: As the snout is a bit big for the giraffe's head, you may find that sewing it on now is a little bit annoying. I prefer the result, but if you're not having a good day, you may want to sew the snout on after you have finished and stuffed the body.

Sew the eyes between rounds 11 and 17, right next to the snout. Embroider the cheeks below the eyes with pastel pink yarn.

Continue in a stripe pattern, alternating 2 rounds in graphite and 2 rounds in off-white yarn. Stuff the head and continue stuffing the neck as you go.
Note: The increases have to be at the center back. If you're not there when starting round 21, add a few more sc or undo a few.
Rnd 21: inc in next st, sc in next 35 st [37]
Note: To keep the color change line straight, you can make the color change above the second sc of each increase stitch.
Rnd 22 – 28: sc in all 37 st [37]
Rnd 29: sc in next st, inc in next st, sc in next 35 st [38]
Rnd 30 – 36: sc in all 38 st [38]
Rnd 37: sc in next 2 st, inc in next st, sc in next 35 st [39]
Rnd 38 – 44: sc in all 39 st [39]
Rnd 45: sc in next 3 st, inc in next st, sc in next 35 st [40]
Rnd 46 – 52: sc in all 40 st [40]
Rnd 53: sc in next 4 st, inc in next st, sc in next 35 st [41]
Rnd 54 – 60: sc in all 41 st [41]

Change to teal green yarn.
Rnd 61: sc in next 5 st, inc in next st, sc in next 35 [42]
Rnd 62: sc in all 42 st [42]

Change to light warm gray yarn.
Rnd 63: BLO sc in all 42 st [42]
Rnd 64: Find the middle back stitch of the body. If you're not there yet, continue crocheting until that point. Then, ch 12. (Place a stitch marker in the next st you make – the first you will make on the foundation chain, this will mark the beginning of the next rounds.) Crochet back on the chain, start in second ch from the hook, sc in next 11 st, sc in the stitch where the foundation chain starts, continue on the body and sc in next 42 st, continue on the other side of the chain and sc in next 10 st, inc in next st [66]
Rnd 65: sc in next st, inc in next st, sc in next 28 st, (inc in next st, sc in next st) repeat 2 times, inc in next st, sc in next 28 st, inc in next st, sc in next st, inc in next st [72]
Rnd 66: inc in next 2 st, sc in next 68 st, inc in next 2 st [76]
Rnd 67: sc in next 2 st, inc in next st, sc in next 69 st, inc in next st, sc in next 3 st [78]
Rnd 68: sc in next 3 st, inc in next st, sc in next 31 st, (inc in next st, sc in next 2 st) repeat 2 times, inc in next st, sc in next 32 st, inc in next st, sc in next 3 st [83]
Rnd 69: inc in next st, sc in next 3 st, inc in next st, sc in next 74 st, inc in next st, sc in next 3 st [86]
Rnd 70 – 81: sc in all 86 st [86]
Do not fasten off.

LEGS

We have to divide the work to crochet the four legs.

FIRST BACK LEG
First, find the middle back stitch of the body. If you are not there yet, continue crocheting until that point. Then, sc in next 3 st. Place a stitch marker in the next stitch. Sc in next 12 st, ch 8. Join the last ch to the stitch with the stitch marker by working a slst.
Continue working the first back leg:
Rnd 1: sc in next 12 on the body, sc in next 8 ch [20]
Rnd 2 – 16: sc in all 20 st [20]

Change to off-white yarn.
Rnd 17 – 21: sc in all 20 st [20]

Change to black yarn.
Rnd 22 – 24: sc in all 20 st [20]
Rnd 25: (sc in next 2 st, dec) repeat 5 times [15]
Rnd 26: (sc in next st, dec) repeat 5 times [10]
Rnd 27: dec 5 times [5]
Fasten off, leaving a long tail. Using a tapestry needle, weave the yarn tail through the front loop of each remain-

ing stitch and pull tight to close. Weave in the yarn end.

FIRST FRONT LEG

Count 13 stitches along from the first back leg (this will become the belly) and pull up a loop of light warm gray yarn in the 14th stitch.
Sc in this st, sc in next 11 st, ch 8 and join the last ch to the first sc stitch with a slst.
Rnd 1 – 27: repeat rounds 1-27 of the first back leg.

SECOND FRONT LEG

Count 6 st to the left of the first front leg (this is the space between the legs) and pull up a loop of light warm gray yarn in the 7th stitch.
Sc in this st, sc in next 11 st, ch 8 and join the last ch to the first sc stitch with a slst.
Rnd 1 – 27: repeat rounds 1-27 of the first back leg.

SECOND BACK LEG

Count 13 st to the left of the second front leg (this is the other side of the belly) and pull up a loop of light warm gray yarn in the 14th stitch.
Sc in this st, sc in next 11 st, ch 8 and join the last ch to the first sc stitch with a slst.
Rnd 1 – 27: repeat rounds 1-27 of the first back leg.

BELLY

Between the legs you now have 13-stitch-spaces along the sides and 6-stitch-spaces at the front and back. Make the belly by crocheting flaps on these stitches. Start with the 13-stitch-space along the side. Pull up a loop of light warm gray yarn in the first stitch next to the first leg you made. Crochet in rows.
Row 1 – 14: sc in next 13 st, ch 1, turn.
Fasten off, leaving a long tail for sewing.

FLAP BETWEEN THE LEGS

For the back flap, pull up a loop of light warm gray yarn in the first stitch next to the last leg you made. Crochet in rows.
Row 1 – 4: sc in next 6 st, ch 1, turn [6]
Fasten off, leaving a long tail for sewing. Work the flap between the front legs in the same way.

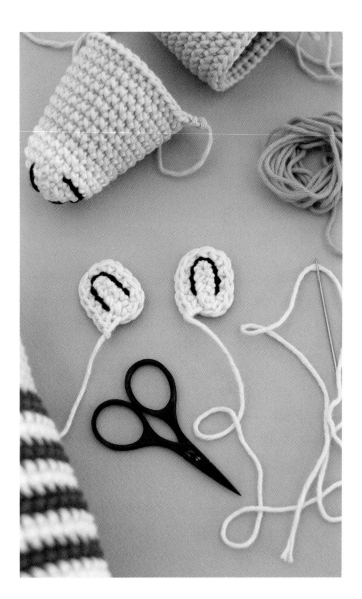

ASSEMBLY OF THE BODY
Using a tapestry needle, sew the front flap to both front legs and the back flap to both back legs. Stuff each leg firmly with fiberfill.
Using a tapestry needle, sew the wide belly flap to the opposite side of the body. Then sew the belly flap to both legs and the flaps between them, stuffing the body as you go.

OUTER EARS

(make 2, in light warm gray)
Rnd 1: start 6 sc in a magic ring [6]
Rnd 2: (sc in next st, inc in next st) repeat 3 times [9]
Rnd 3: (sc in next 2 st, inc in next st) repeat 3 times [12]
Rnd 4: sc in all 12 st [12]
Rnd 5: (sc in next 3 st, inc in next st) repeat 3 times [15]
Rnd 6: sc in all 15 st [15]
Rnd 7: (sc in next 4 st, inc in next st) repeat 3 times [18]
Rnd 8 – 11: sc in all 18 st [18]
Rnd 12: (sc in next st, dec) repeat 6 times [12]
Rnd 13 – 15: sc in all 12 st [12]
Fasten off, leaving a long tail for sewing. Do not stuff.

INNER EARS

(make 2, start in off-white)
Ch 8. Stitches are worked around both sides of the foundation chain.
Rnd 1: start in second ch from the hook, inc in next st, sc in next 5 st, 3 sc in last st. Change to black yarn and continue on the other side of the foundation chain, sc in next st, hdc in next 2 st, dc in next 2 st, hdc in last st [16] Change to off-white yarn, fasten off the black yarn.
Rnd 2: (inc in next st, sc in next 7 st) repeat 2 times [18]
Slst in next st. Fasten off, leaving a long tail for sewing. Sew the inner ear to the inside of the light warm gray ear. Flatten and fold the ears before sewing. Sew the ears between rounds 7 and 10 of the head.

HORNS

(make 2, start in black)
Rnd 1: start 8 sc in a magic ring [8]
Rnd 2 – 3: sc in all 8 st [8]
Change to light warm gray yarn.
Rnd 4 – 11: sc in all 8 st [8]
Fasten off, leaving a long tail for sewing. Stuff the horns lightly. Sew them on the top of the head, above the ears, between rounds 3 and 5.

TAIL

(start in black)
Rnd 1: start 5 sc in a magic ring [5]
Rnd 2 – 3: sc in all 5 st [5]
Change to light warm gray yarn.
Rnd 4 – 6: sc in all 5 st [5]
Fasten off, leaving a long tail for sewing.
Do not stuff. Sew the tail to the back,
centered between rounds 66 and 67.

SPOTS

(make 12, in black)
Rnd 1: start 8 sc in a magic
ring [8]
Fasten off, leaving a long
tail for sewing. Sew the
spots randomly over the
giraffe's body.

Eduardo Cutesaurus

Eduardo is a Diplodocus, but instead of having pointy spikes lining his back, he was born with a colorful mix of rounded spikes, all in different shapes and textures. He was so small and so cute that his great-aunt, the best cake maker in the world, called him "my Eduardo Cutesaurus". Together they made the most colorful textured mini cakes, just like Eduardo's spikes. Now, Eduardo is a full grown dinosaur and has been a pastry chef for years. He is the happiest dinosaur because he opened a pastry shop with his friend Cosmo Snail. And in honor of the best great-aunt to ever have walked the earth, they named the bakery "Aunt Cutie Cakes".

GALLERY: Scan or visit *www.amigurumi.com/4120* to share pictures and find inspiration.

SKILL LEVEL * *

Size:
13.5 inches / 34 cm tall and 14.2 inches / 36 cm long when made with the indicated yarn

Materials:
– Worsted weight yarn in
 · pastel mint (about 200 g in total)
 · off-white
 · pastel pink
 · burnt orange
 · graphite gray
– Size C-2 / 2.75 mm crochet hook
– Black safety eyes (10 mm)
– Tapestry needle
– Fiberfill

Skills needed: magic ring *(page 32)*, working around a foundation chain *(page 34)*, changing color at the beginning of a round *(page 35)*, dividing the body in four parts *(page 160)*, joining parts *(page 39)*, embroidery *(page 38)*

Note: The head, body and legs are worked in one piece.

HEAD AND BODY

(in pastel mint)
Ch 9. Stitches are worked around both sides of the foundation chain.
Rnd 1: start in second ch from the hook, inc in this st, sc in next 6 st, 3 sc in last st. Continue on the other side of the foundation chain, sc in next 7 st [18]
Rnd 2: inc in next 2 st, sc in next 6 st, inc in next 3 st, sc in next 6 st, inc in next st [24]
Rnd 3: (sc in next st, inc in next st) repeat 2 times, sc in next 7 st, (inc in next st, sc in next st) repeat 2 times, inc in next st, sc in next 7 st, inc in next st [30]
Rnd 4: (sc in next st, inc in next st) repeat 3 times, sc in next 8 st, (inc in next st, sc in next st) repeat 3 times, inc in next st, sc in next 8 st, inc in next st [38]
Rnd 5: (inc in next st, sc in next 2 st) repeat 2 times, inc in next st, sc in next 12 st, (inc in next st, sc in next 2 st) repeat 2 times, inc in next st, sc in next 12 st [44]
Rnd 6: (inc in next st, sc in next 3 st) repeat 2 times, inc in next st, sc in next 13 st, (inc in next st, sc in next 3 st) repeat 2 times, inc in next st, sc in next 13 st [50]
Rnd 7: (sc in next 4 st, inc in next st) repeat 10 times [60]
Rnd 8 – 16: sc in all 60 st [60]
Insert the safety eyes between rounds 11 and 12, with and interspace of about 35 stitches at the front. Embroider the cheeks with pastel pink yarn.
Note: The decreases in rounds 17-21 have to be aligned with the front of the dinosaur's head. If necessary, add or undo a few sc to make sure you get the shape right.
Rnd 17: sc in next 24 st, (dec, sc in next 3 st) repeat 5 times, dec, sc in next 9 st [54]

Rnd 18: sc in next 23 st, (dec, sc in next 2 st) repeat 5 times, dec, sc in next 9 st [48]
Rnd 19: (sc in next 6 st, dec) repeat 6 times [42]
Rnd 20: sc in next 19 st, (dec, sc in next st) repeat 5 times, dec, sc in next 6 st [36]
Rnd 21: sc in next 16 st, (dec, sc in next st) repeat 5 times, dec, sc in next 3 st [30]
Rnd 22: (sc in next 3 st, dec) repeat 6 times [24]
Rnd 23: sc in next 15 st, dec, sc in next 3 st, dec, sc in next 2 st [22]
Rnd 24: sc in all 22 st [22]
Stuff the head and continue stuffing the neck as you go.
Rnd 25: sc in next 15 st, inc in next st, sc in next 3 st, inc in next st, sc in next 2 st [24]
Rnd 26 – 28: sc in all 24 st [24]
Rnd 29: sc in next 16 st, inc in next st, sc in next 5 st, inc in next st, sc in next st [26]
Rnd 30 – 32: sc in all 26 st [26]
Rnd 33: sc in next 17 st, inc in next st, sc in next 6 st, inc in next st, sc in next st [28]
Rnd 34 – 36: sc in all 28 st [28]
Rnd 37: sc in next 5 st, inc in next st, sc in next 3 st, inc in next st, sc in next 8 st, inc in next st, sc in next 7 st, inc in next st, sc in next st [32]
Rnd 38 – 40: sc in all 32 st [32]
Rnd 41: sc in next 6 st, inc in next st, sc in next 4 st, inc in next st, sc in next 9 st, inc in next st, sc in next 8 st, inc in next st, sc in next st [36]
Rnd 42 – 46: sc in all 36 st [36]
Rnd 47: Find the middle back of the body. If you're not there yet, continue crocheting until that point (I had to crochet 11 sc to get there). Then, ch 15. (Place a stitch marker in the next st you make – the first you will make on the foundation chain, this will mark the beginning of the next rounds.) Crochet back on the chain, inc in second ch from the hook, sc in next 13 st, sc in the stitch where the foundation chain starts, continue on the body and sc in next 12 st, inc in next st, sc in next 9 st, inc in next st, sc in next 13 st, continue on the other side of the chain and sc in next 14 st [68]

Rnd 48: inc in next 2 st, sc in next 65 st, inc in next st [71]
Rnd 49: (sc in next st, inc in next st) repeat 2 times, sc in next 66 st, inc in next st [74]
Rnd 50: (sc in next 2 st, inc in next st) repeat 2 times, sc in next 27 st, inc in next st, sc in next 10 st, inc in next st, sc in next 28 st, inc in next st [79]
Rnd 51: sc in next 2 st, inc in next st, sc in next 3 st, inc in next st, sc in next 70 st, inc in next st, sc in next st [82]
Rnd 52: sc in next st, (inc in next st, sc in next 2 st) repeat 2 times, inc in next st, sc in next 72 st, inc in next st, sc in next st [86]
Rnd 53 – 68: sc in all 86 st [86]
Do not fasten off.

LEGS

We have to divide the work to crochet the four legs.

FIRST BACK LEG
First, find the middle back stitch of the body. If you are not there yet, continue crocheting until that point. Then, sc in next 2 st. Place a stitch marker in the next stitch. Sc in next 13 st, ch 8. Join the last ch to the stitch with the stitch marker by working a slst.
Continue working the first back leg:
Rnd 1: sc in next 13 st on the body, sc in next 8 ch [21]
Rnd 2 – 12: sc in all 21 st [21]
Rnd 13: (sc in next st, dec) repeat 7 times [14]
Rnd 14: dec 7 times [7]
Fasten off, leaving a long tail. Using a tapestry needle, weave the yarn tail through the front loop of each remaining stitch and pull tight to close. Weave in the yarn end.

FIRST FRONT LEG
Count 13 stitches along from the first back leg (this will

become the belly) and pull up a loop of pastel mint yarn in the 14th stitch.
Sc in this st, sc in next 12 st, ch 8 and join the last ch to the first sc stitch with a slst.
Rnd 1 – 14: repeat rounds 1-14 of the first back leg.

SECOND FRONT LEG

Count 4 st to the left of the first front leg (this is the space between the legs) and pull up a loop of pastel mint yarn in the 5th stitch.
Sc in this st, sc in next 12 st, ch 8 and join the last ch to the first sc stitch with a slst.
Rnd 1 – 14: repeat rounds 1-14 of the first back leg.

SECOND BACK LEG

Count 13 st to the left of the second front leg (this is the other side of the belly) and pull up a loop of pastel mint yarn in the 14th stitch.
Sc in this st, sc in next 12 st, ch 8 and join the last ch to the first sc stitch with a slst.
Rnd 1 – 14: repeat rounds 1-14 of the first back leg.

BELLY

Between the legs you have 13-stitch-spaces along the sides and 4-stitch-spaces at the front and back.
We make the belly by crocheting flaps on these stitches.
Start with the 13-stitch-space along the side. Pull up a loop of pastel mint yarn in the first stitch next to the first leg you made. Crochet in rows.
Row 1 – 12: sc in next 13 st, ch 1, turn [13]
Fasten off, leaving a long tail for sewing.

FLAP BETWEEN THE LEGS

For the back flap, pull up a loop of pastel mint yarn in the first stitch next to the last leg you made. Crochet in rows.
Row 1 – 4: sc in next 4 st, ch 1, turn [4]
Fasten off, leaving a long tail for sewing. Work the flap

between the front legs in the same way.

ASSEMBLY OF THE BODY

Using a tapestry needle, sew the front flap to both front legs and the back flap to both back legs.
Stuff each leg firmly with fiberfill.
Using a tapestry needle, sew the wide belly flap to the opposite side of the body. Then sew the belly flap to both legs and the flaps between them, stuffing the body as you go.

TAIL

(in pastel mint)
Rnd 1: start 6 sc in a magic ring [6]
Rnd 2: sc in all 6 st [6]
Rnd 3: (sc in next st, inc in next st) repeat 3 times [9]
Rnd 4 – 5: sc in all 9 st [9]
Rnd 6: (sc in next 2 st, inc in next st) repeat 3 times [12]
Rnd 7 – 8: sc in all 12 st [12]
Rnd 9: (sc in next 3 st, inc in next st) repeat 3 times [15]
Rnd 10 – 11: sc in all 15 st [15]
Rnd 12: (sc in next 4 st, inc in next st) repeat 3 times [18]
Rnd 13 – 14: sc in all 18 st [18]
Rnd 15: (sc in next 5 st, inc in next st) repeat 3 times [21]

Rnd 16 – 17: sc in all 21 st [21]
Rnd 18: (sc in next 6 st, inc in next st) repeat 3 times [24]
Rnd 19 – 20: sc in all 24 st [24]
Rnd 21: (sc in next 7 st, inc in next st) repeat 3 times [27]
Rnd 22 – 23: sc in all 27 st [27]
Rnd 24: (sc in next 8 st, inc in next st) repeat 3 times [30]
Rnd 25 – 26: sc in all 30 st [30]
Rnd 27: (sc in next 9 st, inc in next st) repeat 3 times [33]
Rnd 28 – 29: sc in all 33 st [33]
Rnd 30: (sc in next 10 st, inc in next st) repeat 3 times [36]
Rnd 31 – 32: sc in all 36 st [36]
Rnd 33: (sc in next 11 st, inc in next st) repeat 3 times [39]
Rnd 34 – 35: sc in all 39 st [39]
Rnd 36: (sc in next 12 st, inc in next st) repeat 3 times [42]
Rnd 37 – 38: sc in all 42 st [42]
Rnd 39: (sc in next 13 st, inc in next st) repeat 3 times [45]
Rnd 40 – 41: sc in all 45 st [45]
Fasten off, leaving a long tail for sewing. Stuff with fiberfill. Sew the tail centered to the dino's back.

SPIKES

EXTRA SMALL
(make 5: 1 in pastel pink, 1 in pale pink, 1 graphite and off-white striped and 2 in burnt orange)
Rnd 1: start 8 sc in a magic ring [8]
Rnd 2 – 4: sc in all 8 st [8]
Fasten off, leaving a long tail for sewing.

SMALL
(make 6, 1 graphite and off-white striped, 1 in pale pink, 1 in burnt orange and 3 in pastel pink)
Rnd 1: start 6 sc in a magic ring [6]
Rnd 2: inc in all 6 st [12]
Rnd 3 – 6: sc in all 12 st [12]
Fasten off, leaving a long tail for sewing.

MEDIUM
(make 3, 1 in burnt orange and 2 in pale pink)
Rnd 1: start 6 sc in a magic ring [6]
Rnd 2: inc in all 6 st [12]
Rnd 3: (sc in next st, inc in next st) repeat 6 times [18]
Rnd 4 – 6: sc in all 18 st [18]
Fasten off, leaving a long tail for sewing.

LARGE
(make 2, 1 in burnt orange and 1 in pastel pink)
Rnd 1: start 8 sc in a magic ring [8]
Rnd 2: inc in all 8 st [16]
Rnd 3 – 8: sc in all 16 st [16]
Fasten off, leaving a long tail for sewing.

EXTRA LARGE
(make 1, start in graphite)
Rnd 1: start 6 sc in a magic ring [6]
Change to off-white.
Rnd 2: inc in all 6 st [12]
Continue in a stripe pattern, alternating graphite and off-white yarn.
Rnd 3: (sc in next st, inc in next st) repeat 6 times [18]
Rnd 4 – 10: sc in all 18 st [18]
Fasten off, leaving a long tail for sewing.

ASSEMBLY OF THE SPIKES
Position the spikes on the Cutesaurus' back. The Extra large and large spikes are positioned next to the neck, followed by a mix of medium and small spikes and finally position the extra small spikes at the end of the tail. Sew them on, using the yarn tails.

Thanks to those who help me keep going and care about me, even
though I can be a little quirky at times...well, most of the time.
I love you. Live long and prosper.